children's parties

rose hammick
charlotte packer

children's parties

fun ideas for fabulous kids' parties   recipes by caroline marson

RYLAND
PETERS
& SMALL
LONDON NEW YORK

photography by
polly wreford

First published in the United Kingdom
in 2006. This paperback edition
published in 2009 by
Ryland Peters & Small
20–21 Jockey's Fields
London WC1R 4BW
www.rylandpeters.com

10 9 8 7 6 5 4 3 2 1

ISBN: 978-1-84597-824-2

Printed and bound in China

Senior designer Catherine Griffin
Senior editor Annabel Morgan
Picture research Emily Westlake
Production manager Patricia Harrington
Art director Anne-Marie Bulat
Publishing director Alison Starling

Stylist Rose Hammick
Text Charlotte Packer

To Matilda, Beatrice, Martha and Joe – C.P.
To Blaise and Andrew – R.H.

contents

introduction

Most of us look back fondly at the birthday parties of our childhood – simple celebrations involving a party tea, occasional fancy dress, and an afternoon of games. The highlight of the party was a cake, almost always home-made and not always very good! And that was all we expected. In those days, party bags and entertainers were rare, and few parents sent children home with anything other than a slice of cake. Just the prospect of winning a few games was enough to keep us happy, though of course there were always tears – on that front, at least, nothing has changed!

These days, however, when it comes to children's parties, many of us have lost the confidence to do it ourselves, so we throw money at the problem instead. But it doesn't have to be this way. First of all children's expectations are often lower than we imagine and, with a little ingenuity and basic planning, kids are not difficult to entertain. A simple fancy-dress theme, with a few appropriate decorations, is all it takes to get children's imaginations working and, before you know it, an hour has passed with everyone happily pretending to be knights, princesses, fairies or pirates. Add some

CLOCKWISE FROM ABOVE LEFT Gingham bunting, a few bales of straw and some cardboard cacti transform an urban back garden into the Wild West; a jokey hand-painted strongman photo panel is the perfect prop for a circus party; a pirate scans the horizon from a climbing-frame pirate galleon; two little cowboys plot their escape from a playhouse jail!

party food (shop bought or home-made, whichever
keeps your blood pressure down) and a few good
games, and you're home and dry.

To make life a little easier (we hope), all the
parties in this book were conceived to suit both
those who enjoy the challenge of getting to grips
with cardboard and glue and those who can't think
of anything worse. Every theme includes ideas for
home-made decorations and costumes, as well as
versions that can be bought and customized if time
is short or creativity is not your thing. Party plans for
each age group offer alternative party ideas, and

suggestions for food, games and activities, while
there are separate chapters covering home-made
invitations, party games and party bags. Part two is
all about the food and, as well as a comprehensive
selection of recipes to suit all tastes and ages, there
are fun suggestions for birthday cakes.

If on the day the inevitable chaos overwhelms
you, remember that, although our children's parties
may feel a world away from those of our childhood,
the ingredients for a great birthday party are
unchanged – friends, games and cake. And if you've
got those your child's friends will go home happy!

the parties

The themes on the following pages are designed to inspire you, not pressurize you! This section is not about how children's parties *should* be, more about how they *could* be, if yours is the sort of family that enjoys fancy dress and creating make-believe worlds. The decorative schemes are necessarily lavish in order to show all that can be made for each theme. But, in every instance, the look can be established through costumes or decorations alone. It is up to you how far you wish to take things, and enjoyment should be the deciding factor. If your child hates dressing up, or if you don't have the time to make decorations, don't worry. Parties are about more than just the way a room looks. Remember: a delicious cake and an afternoon having fun with their closest friends is the perfect way to celebrate your child's birthday.

OPPOSITE PAGE Creating a pretty picnic spot is easy and as simple as placing a rug and a few comfy cushions in the shade of a tree. Here, a child's play tent has been festooned with festive gingham bunting to provide the focus for the birthday tea.

BELOW AND RIGHT Be warned that at this age not all the children will be interested in sitting down for tea, so have a few simple activities close at hand to keep them occupied, such as brick trolleys and dolls' buggies or a sandpit to play in. Although this age group is too young for traditional party games, you could hide a few small toys in the sandpit and help them to dig for buried treasure.

First and second birthday parties may mean more to the parents than they do to the children themselves, but a teddy bears' picnic is an ideal celebration for this age group.

teddy bears' picnic

In the early years, birthday parties can be surprisingly large affairs: not only do they involve the other children's parents but, more often than not, a sprinkling of older siblings as well. Although your child may seem too young to know what's going on, a simple theme such as a teddy bears' picnic is a good idea. Every child has a teddy bear or stuffed animal, and a picnic with toys will also appeal to any older children you have invited.

If the weather permits, hold the party in the garden or a nearby park – not only is an outdoor setting more appropriate for a picnic, but it will also save your house from an invasion of rampaging toddlers with sticky fingers. You can gear most of the food to adult tastes, but make sure you have a small selection of easy finger food for the babies – little sandwiches with the crusts cut off, breadsticks, chunky sticks of cucumber and carrot and cherry tomatoes all go down well with the under-twos.

In terms of decoration, a teddy bears' picnic is a breeze and can be as simple or full-on as you wish. A picnic blanket and a few cushions is enough to set the scene, and bunting, which looks very

RIGHT The birthday cake is central to a child's big day, and a thick layer of brightly coloured butter icing and a generous sprinkling of sweets are all you need to give your child a cake to remember (the icing is all they're really interested in, anyway!).

OPPOSITE PAGE A troupe of teddy bears marching through the flowerbeds makes a great party decoration. Each bear has been cut from stiff brown card and has a contrasting lighter patch glued to its tummy. The bears are mounted on bamboo canes. Paint each guest's name onto a bear, and give them out as going-home presents.

jolly and is easy to make (or buy), will add an instant sense of festivity. To make your own bunting, either cut sheets of brightly coloured tissue paper into triangles of roughly the same size and glue them at regular intervals to lengths of string, or sew triangular fabric scraps to lengths of ribbon using the zigzag stitch on a sewing machine. You can use the bunting to decorate your garden or, if you decide to hold the party in a local park, to demarcate your picnic area and make it easier for your guests to spot the festivities from a distance.

Toddler-sized cut-outs of friendly-looking teddy bears make effective and very simple decorations, and can be used for both indoor and outdoor parties. The cut-out bears can either be stuck to walls near the tea table or, as at this party, mounted on bamboo canes and set up so they appear to be strolling through the flowerbeds. Cut out a simple teddy bear template, then draw round the outline on stiff brown card. Once you have cut out enough teddies, stick patches of paler

if you go down to the woods today... Some children may forget to bring a teddy bear and end up feeling left out if everyone else has one. To avoid squabbles over another child's favourite bear, it's a good idea to put out as many soft toys as you can to ensure that everyone has a toy to play with.

THIS PAGE AND RIGHT
Juice in tiny tea-cups is perfect for a teddy bears' picnic, as long as you are relaxed about the inevitable spills. You may decide that the tea set is best used as a 'let's pretend' game with all the guests' teddies before the real tea is served.

RIGHT, ABOVE AND BELOW Look for teddy-shaped biscuits or crisps in the shops, or make and ice your own (see page 129). Animal-shaped cutters are widely available, and you can let your children help with the decorating as a fun pre-party activity. The flower biscuits are made using melted boiled sweets (see page 128).

brown paper onto their tummies (add more patches for paws and a nose, if you want to). These cut-outs can also form the basis of a fun craft activity for older children – sit them at tables equipped with glue, glitter, paints and tissue paper, and set them to work decorating their own teddy to take home with them.

If you have a play tent or playhouse, put it into use as part of the scenery, and add any other toys you have that either tie in with the theme or provide good outdoor entertainment. A dolls' tea set is an obvious choice, as is any plastic play food. Older children will be quick to start serving the toys with tea, while the toddlers will no doubt infuriate them by refusing to participate properly! Toy strollers, dolls' buggies and wooden trikes are all popular with toddlers, and are perfect for ferrying teddy bears up and down the garden. Sandpits will entertain children of any age (and make great first birthday presents), and for a simple, low-key party game you could bury plastic animals or little cars or play figures in the sand, then encourage the children to dig them up again.

With a baby- and toddler-friendly party theme like this, you shouldn't have too much trouble keeping the children happy, as they will largely occupy themselves, which means that you'll have a more relaxing and enjoyable time, too!

LEFT Fancy dress is a little too complicated for toddlers, but cute animal ears are just right, especially as little ones love trying on hats.

RIGHT AND OPPOSITE PAGE These pretty waterlilies were made by glueing tissue-paper petals to paper jelly bowls (available in supermarkets) and placing them on lily pads cut from sheets of plain green paper.

A party based on simple, familiar motifs such as farm animals, combined with simple activities and singing, is ideal for little ones. Decorate your space with colourful outsize decorations to ensure a memorable celebration.

farmyard animals

Although it's nice to host your child's birthday party at home, a local community centre or school hall is an excellent alternative if you are obliged to invite the whole of your child's class at playgroup or nursery, if your home is particularly small, or if you have a large extended family.

The only downside is that these community spaces tend to be rather impersonal or even drab-looking. However they can be cheered up quite easily with simple home-made decorations based around favourite stories, animals or toys from home.

Devise your scheme according to how much time you are prepared to give to it, and also bear in mind practicalities, such as how you will transport and set up any decorations that you make. A dull hall can be given an instant lift with balloons, streamers and tables of party food. But if you really enjoy the challenge, the transformation of your local hall is limited only by your imagination, and with a little lateral thinking a really memorable and highly personal celebration shouldn't cost more than many people spend on a party session at a fast-food chain.

OPPOSITE PAGE Babies and toddlers love pottering about and investigating the world around them. Here, comfy gingham cushions are perfect for tumbling around on, while the numerous toy animals provide entertainment. They could also double as going-home treats.

OPPOSITE PAGE A selection of simple musical instruments, such as tambourines, drums and shakers, is all that you need in the way of entertainment for two-year-olds. Get them out at a suitable moment, such as just before tea, and let the children make as much noise as they like!

THIS PAGE, INSET BELOW The cut-out farm animals were copied from favourite picture books and painted onto stiff paper. They were then cut out and dotted around the room.

Although the decorations for this farmyard party look lavish, in fact almost all were either home-made, or toys that were adapted to serve as props. Only a few items, such as the giant flowers and butterflies, were bought and they were chosen not only for their decorative value but also so they could be handed out as going-home presents – cheap, charming and welcome additions to the departing guests' bedrooms.

The playhouse (which looks just like a picture-book farmhouse) and a collection of plastic rabbits were the starting point for the farmyard theme. A low picket fence, cut from cardboard and then sprayed blue, and some animals, which were painted onto cheap lining paper, were all it took to transform the room into a fabulous farmyard. The nice thing about creating decorations for this age group is that their charm lies in their simplicity, so you don't need to be particularly skilled with a pencil or paintbrush.

The plump gingham cushions are the sort of thing a child might have in their bedroom or playroom, and are perfect for toddlers to roll about on. They can also form a suitable area for any circle activities, such as singing, that you might be planning.

There is no point trying to organize a fancy dress party for this age group, as most children will resist costumes vigorously, but under-twos do love trying on all kinds of headgear, from woolly bobble hats to policemen's helmets, so cute animal ears are sure to

think about the little things Set up a changing station for babies with a mat, wipes and nappies for mums who may have forgotten them. A potty for toilet-training toddlers is another good idea.

appeal. Either make your own by sewing shaped pieces of velvet or fake fur together and attaching them to hairbands, or buy them from a party shop. These also make lovely going-home presents.

If the hall is large, treat the space as you might a playgroup and set up various activities around the room, each one geared to the various age groups attending. The duck pond, made from sheets of blue paper taped together and cut to create wavy edges, not only looks wonderful but is also part of a magnetic fishing game for toddlers. The ducks have nails hammered into their bases and can be caught using the fishing rods, which have small magnets (from hardware shops) at the ends of their lines.

This sort of party is ideal for large groups with mixed ages, as it caters both for children who still want a lot of interaction from their parents as well as those who will simply want to crash about with their friends. It'll be noisy – but great fun.

LEFT A child's cardboard playhouse is decorated with flowers made from paper jelly bowls and tissue petals.

THIS PICTURE AND FAR RIGHT A fun fishing game was made by customizing a family of rubber ducks, while a few plastic caterpillars do duty as bait. Nails were hammered into the bases of the ducks and small magnets were glued to the caterpillars, which were then tied to bamboo rods. The aim of the game is to see how many ducks you can hook out of the pond. Three- and four-year-olds will love this, and so will younger children, but they may need a helping hand.

party plan

Let's be honest – first and second birthday parties are often seized upon by first-time parents as a rare chance to throw a party for themselves. And why not? Your one- or two-year-old won't have any idea about (let alone say in) who gets invited, but will love the attention. Throw a fun family-oriented party with food to suit adults and simple finger foods for little ones, who will no doubt be in the minority.

WHERE SHALL WE HAVE IT?
• Where you host the party depends upon what you plan to do. If you want to hold your party at home, Sunday brunch or a barbecue are both nice ways to celebrate a child's birthday, while also catering for the adult contingent.
• A trip to the park is great if your home is small and you have friends who'll be coming along with several children in tow.

WHAT'S THE BEST TIME?
• Many children in this age group still have a daytime nap. Organize your party to suit your child's routine. Don't be brow-beaten by parents who sigh and say, well of course we'd love to come, but that's when little Johnny has his nap (the barely veiled inference being that perhaps you could change the time to suit them). It's your party – do it your way.
• How long can you face being the host? Two hours with full-on toddler antics in your own home can feel like a lifetime. However, if your party is in the garden or a park, you may want it to run on all afternoon.
• If you've hired a venue, you will probably be restricted by hourly rates. Remember to factor in time to set up at the beginning and clear up at the end.

WHAT FOOD SHOULD WE SERVE?
• Generally, parties for this age group involve catering for adults as well as children. If you are organizing a barbecue or picnic, provide chicken drumsticks and burgers (see pages 116–117) as well as salads. For the babies, simple finger food, such as little sandwiches and cocktail sausages, is ideal.
• Before you go overboard working out what to cook for your friends, remember that most adults have a secret fondness for cocktail sausages, crisps and child-sized sandwiches. You could save yourself a lot of time and effort by simply treating the adults as children and catering accordingly.
• Fairy cakes and biscuits always go down well, and so much the better if they are home-made – parents feel far more anxious about what their under-threes eat.
• For the adults, a Sunday brunch of smoked salmon bagels and Buck's fizz, or coffee and muffins, is easy to throw together.

PRIZES AND PARTY BAGS
• Keep these really simple. Give away decorations, such as large paper flowers, which parents can put up in their children's bedrooms.
• Toddlers love blown-up rubber or helium balloons, which provide them with hours of entertainment.
• Home-made playdough is a fun going-home present. Put it in little baby-food jars and add a label bearing the recipe, too. To make playdough, combine 1 cup plain flour, 1 cup water, ½ cup salt, 1 tablespoon vegetable oil, 1 teaspoon cream of tartar and 1 tablespoon food colouring in a heavy-based pan over a medium heat. Stir as the mixture thickens and, when it comes together as a dough, remove from the heat. When cool enough to handle, knead the mixture for a minute or two and it's ready.

Experiment with food colouring: 1–2 teaspoons will produce pale, pastel shades, while half a bottle of food colouring or more will give deep, dark colours.

GAMES AND ACTIVITIES

First birthdays

• With one-year olds and their parents in attendance, you don't need anything other than a selection of toys to hand to keep the children entertained.

Second birthdays

• For a party with a group of preschoolers, it's a good idea to create a small play area (inside or out) stocked with a selection of your child's toys.

• For a summer birthday, make giant ice cubes with plastic toys embedded in them. Save yoghurt pots or margarine tubs, and place a small toy in each one. Fill with water and then place the tubs in the freezer until they are frozen solid. Take the blocks out and set them on a tray in the garden. Small children are intrigued by these slippery cubes, and will enjoy trying to extract the toys as the ice melts.

• By the age of two, most children have encountered playdough, and rolling it out and pressing it into moulds provides them with hours of fun. Set up this activity at a child's table or on the floor.

• Circle songs are the closest that this age group can get to playing an organized game. If your guests attend nurseries or go to toddler groups, this will be a familiar activity, and everyone will enjoy joining in. Make shakers for the children using old drinks bottles filled with dried lentils, rice, pasta or sand.

• If the weather is good, a paddling pool with a few centimetres of water in it is fun for children, as is a sandpit. You will find that there is very little that you need to do other than have some towels on hand to dry children off at the end.

A mysterious, watery wonderland is lots of fun to create. Take the colours of the sea as your starting point, and look for fabric, tissue paper and other props in greens for seaweed, turquoise and blue for the sea, and pinks and yellows for the sand and coral.

under the sea

An impressive underwater world is easy to create if you use a mixture of sea-themed props from around the house (you'll be surprised by how many you have) and a few simple, home-made decorations. Round up all the fish-related toys you can, as well as anything made from netting, such as toy nets or laundry bags. With these simple items, you're halfway towards creating the perfect setting for a gathering of beautiful mermaids and shiny sea monsters.

For this under-the-sea theme, we dressed the room with a mixture of decorations made specially for the party and simple household items such as a child's table and a netting toy store, which were adapted to great effect. The green netting toy store was hung from the ceiling and is a quirky way to display going-home presents, while a large cotton net (used for balloon drops and available from party shops) was decorated with plastic fish to resemble a deep-sea fishing net.

Streamers made from lengths of pale blue and green tissue paper were strung across the ceiling to give the impression of seaweedy fronds waving underwater. Shoals of fish, made from cardboard covered with silver foil and hung from cotton thread, were suspended in groups around the room.

The costumes for this party offer lots of choice. For girls, mermaids are always popular, and costumes are widely available. For boys, a deep-sea diver's outfit can be conjured up out of black

ABOVE For mermaids' wigs, cut lining paper into strips and sew together along a central parting on a sewing machine (or use sticky tape). Finish with a rough application of yellow paint and a sprinkling of gold stars.

ABOVE RIGHT Bath toys can be pressed into service as decorations; here rubber fish have been 'caught' in a large net (these are usually used for balloon drops and are available from good party shops).

RIGHT A toy storage net is the perfect place to stash going-home treats.

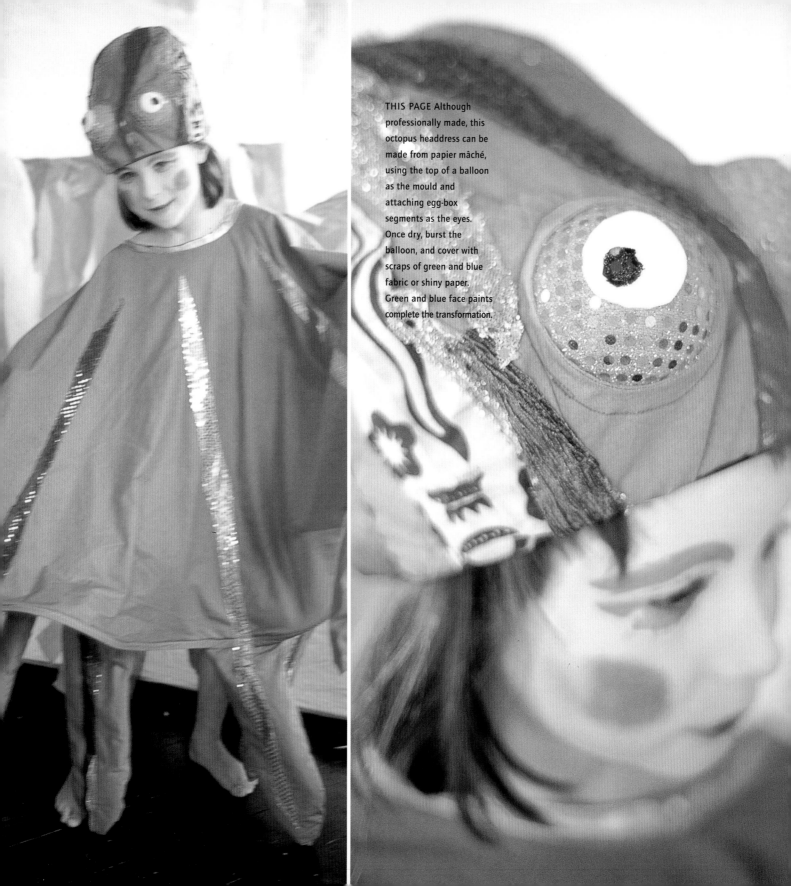

THIS PAGE Although professionally made, this octopus headdress can be made from papier mâché, using the top of a balloon as the mould and attaching egg-box segments as the eyes. Once dry, burst the balloon, and cover with scraps of green and blue fabric or shiny paper. Green and blue face paints complete the transformation.

THIS PAGE Create a shoal of silvery fish by cutting fish shapes from sheets of iridescent card or, as in this case, thin plastic, and then suspend them on fine thread. They look fantastic bobbing about above the tea table.

INSET RIGHT AND BELOW RIGHT Children will love diving in and out of an underwater cave made from a children's play tent that has been covered with strips of blue and green tissue paper seaweed. To create something similar to the sparkly tails of these professionally made costumes (below right), cut a length of suitable fabric into a tail shape and attach ribbon to the top, so that the tail can be tied around the waist.

leggings and top and a rubber mask. If you can't find child-sized flippers, make them from cardboard. For something a little more creative, a jolly Jellyfish is fun to put together. A see-through or pale-coloured umbrella makes a realistic body, and can be combined with pale leggings and a top. For the tentacles, cut pale fabric into long strips, or use lengths of cellophane (or even bubble wrap) and suspend them from the edges of the umbrella. A squid or an octopus could be made in the same way.

A scattering of shells on a turquoise or yellow plastic tablecloth is an effective way to continue the underwater theme at the tea table, or with a little effort you can create something more dramatic. Sand is an obvious (though messy!) addition, and gritty sandwiches are not what you want at a party. However, it's relatively easy to

LEFT A coral crown is the perfect accessory for a mer-queen or the birthday girl. This one was made from paper mâché built up over a wire frame. Once dry, it was painted with pearlescent paint and sprinkled with glitter, sequins and shells.

RIGHT Paper plates have been spray-painted silver to make 'shell' place cards.

BELOW Little cakes (see page 135) decorated with

seaside motifs offer a pretty alternative to a traditional birthday cake. If you don't have time to make the cake, but you enjoy icing, cut up a shop-bought Madeira cake and do your own decorations.

OPPOSITE PAGE Fish-shaped place mats and seaweed streamers are simple yet charming ways to translate a fancy dress theme to the tea table.

seaside snaps Photo-frame plastic snowshakers, which contain glitter-filled water and a slot for a photograph, make perfect going-home presents for this party. If you have a digital or Polaroid camera, take each child's picture as they arrive and print it out during the party, so you can hand each child their snowshaker as they leave.

create a table-top beach by coating a sheet of cardboard or MDF painted yellow with a mixture of sand and PVA glue. Complete the beach scene with miniature sandcastles made by painting individual segments from an egg box with the same mixture. Just add a little flag bearing the guest's name to each sandcastle to turn them into fun place cards. (Although these may seem rather grown-up for this age group, place cards can be a neat way to mix up children who don't know one another well.)

Bright seaside buckets filled with crisps and popcorn make fun alternatives to bowls, as do plastic sand moulds, which can be used for jellies or filled with sweets and biscuits. Alternatively, look for plain paper plates in bright turquoise, blue or yellow, any of which would be perfect for an underwater table.

And, finally, helium balloons in pale watery colours look pretty bobbing around the room like bubbles and can be pulled down from the ceiling or untied from the backs of chairs at the end of the party, to give to guests as they leave.

RIGHT AND CENTRE RIGHT Hand out tiaras as each child arrives, or give them out as prizes for the games (though you will have to make sure that each child manages to 'win' one!).

BOTTOM RIGHT These star cookies on sticks make edible fairy wands. They were baked using a special tin from a cake-decorating supplier and make great going-home presents as the little fairies depart!

OPPOSITE A fairy bower is an essential part of any fairy game! Here, a child's bed canopy has been decorated with tissue paper butterflies attached with dots of washable glue.

Little girls always leap at the chance to dress up as fairies. The costumes are so easy – not only do most girls have a fairy outfit of some form already, but improvising with netting and a pretty party dress is just as good. As for the decorations, just think pink!

fairies

Of all the parties you could arrange for your daughter, a fairy party is probably the easiest – you'll find that you will already have much of what you need, or it will be widely available in high-street stores. Start with a quick trawl of your child's bedroom. Pink cushions, fairy lights, a princess-style mosquito net canopy designed to go over the bed, a butterfly mobile or a pretty rug – all can be pressed into service as party decorations.

Think about the games you might play at a fairy party, and where you will play them, then concentrate your efforts on creating a 'fairy bower'. If your daughter has a summer birthday and you have a garden, then rig up a bower in one corner. Throw down a soft rug, arrange some cushions in a ring, string up a length of pink and white bunting and some pastel-coloured balloons, and you will have created a fairy paradise. If you don't have access to a garden, or the party is in the middle of winter, don't worry – a fairy bower is just as easy to achieve indoors as out. Simply set everything up in the most party-friendly space in the house.

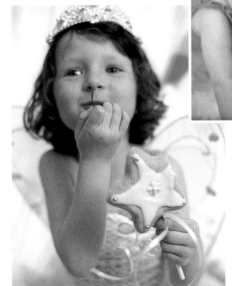

35

THIS PAGE AND INSET LEFT Set the tea table with a pretty tablecloth, and team with plates and cups with floral patterns or in pastel shades. A cake stand piled with fairy cakes makes a sweet focal point. If you want to take the theme further, cut out butterfly shapes from tissue paper and stick them to windows or walls with a dab of glue or a burst of spray mount. A fairy tea without sweets would not feel quite right, but first offer plates of heart-shaped sandwiches with a selection of healthy fillings (see page 114) before letting your little fairies loose on the marshmallows and iced gems!

OPPOSITE PAGE, ABOVE Decorating balloons with tissue-paper butterflies requires no glue as static holds them in place.

OPPOSITE PAGE, BELOW Heart-shaped sandwiches, jellies in flower-shaped moulds and magical sweets are just the things for a fairy tea party.

abracadabra! Slightly older children will enjoy an organized activity in keeping with the party theme, such as wand-making or decorating fairy crowns. It's best to prepare the crown shapes and the sticks and stars for the wands in advance, and then help the children to assemble and decorate them with lots of glittery bits.

Fairy lights always lend a magical, celebratory air to any room, which is just the right effect for a fairy party. Dig out your Christmas tree lights, or look through the shops or mail-order catalogues for slightly more ornate lights (they are now available in a variety of designs such as flowers, butterflies, dragonflies and even fairies). To take the decorations one step further, cut clouds of butterflies from pink, white and purple tissue paper and stick them to windows, curtains and walls or even onto balloons (where static alone will hold them in place).

As the fairy bower will be the central focus of the party, think carefully about where you are going to position it. If you plan to play lots of energetic games, such as Musical Bumps (see page 102), or you are going to have a fairy disco, it may be better to position it in the corner of your largest room, where it will provide a place for children to sit down if they want a rest or as they are eliminated from the games. But if you are planning mostly quiet or circle games, you will need to create a fairy ring large enough for all the children to play in.

Serving a fairy feast in their bower will certainly go down well with children, but it could get messy! It's easy to create a tea table that looks the part. If you can find paper plates, cups and a tablecloth in the same sugary pinks as the balloons and other decorations, you are halfway there. Just add more butterflies, or create simple paper chains to adorn the walls and windows, and let the party food do the rest. Cake stands laden with fairy cakes (see page 130), plates piled with sandwiches cut into hearts, butterflies and flower shapes (see page 114) and dishes of suitably sugary-looking sweets will all make your little fairies very happy indeed.

Once you've planned the overall look of the party, all that's left are the costumes, which you will most probably have the beginnings of already (as will most of the guests). If your daughter doesn't already own a pair of fairy wings, then perhaps these could be a birthday present. As for the dress, you can either embellish her prettiest, most girly party dress with fabric flowers and swathes of net and tulle, or adapt a ballet costume. Sparkly tiaras and wands are the obvious fairy accessories, and these are readily available from most toy and party shops, or are easy to make in an afternoon at home.

ABOVE LEFT, LEFT AND RIGHT You may find that you don't need to arrange many games for fairies: a pretty fairy bower is quite enough to set the mood, and their imaginations will take care of the rest. Younger siblings may not really understand what is going on, but they will certainly want to join in.

ABOVE RIGHT Ready-iced fairy cakes are available in many supermarkets and patisseries, and look every bit as appealing as the home-made versions, especially when presented on a dainty cake stand. The addition of these pretty wired butterfly decorations adds a little extra magic!

THIS PAGE Home-made costumes have a charm all of their own – here, a pretty flower-sprigged vest looks perfect with a ruffled net skirt. Make fairy wands using ribbon and garden canes. Staple one end of the ribbon to the bottom of the can and then wind the ribbon around the cane, glueing carefully as you go, and secure with a staple at the top. Attach a cardboard star (covered with tin foil) to the end of the wand with glue and a staple, and tie streamers to the top to hide the staples.

OPPOSITE PAGE, LEFT AND RIGHT A climbing frame makes an excellent starting point for a pirate galleon sailing the high seas. The sail was made from an old curtain (but you could use a dustsheet or old bedspread) painted with poster paint mixed with a little PVA glue (this works out cheaper than fabric paints, which are expensive and only come in small quantities). The flags and Jolly Roger balloons came from a party shop, and the bunting was made from sheets of black and white fabric cut into triangles and sewn onto string. The black bunting triangles were decorated using a home-made skull-and-crossbones stencil.

A swashbuckling adventure on the high seas need not be merely the stuff of story books – with a little lateral thinking, you can make it happen at home!

pirates

BELOW Pirate costumes are easy to concoct, and even the most self-conscious child can be persuaded to don a pair of cut-off jeans and a stripy T-shirt.

Nothing says 'pirates' quite so powerfully as a Jolly Roger flag, so if making decorations is not your thing, a visit to any local party shop will provide you with plenty of pirate flags and enough black balloons to set the mood for a great pirate party. The children's costumes will do the rest.

However, if you like the challenge of a creative project, and you have a climbing frame, treehouse or even a garden shed, you can provide the children with their own pirate ship or desert-island hideaway! Again, the Jolly Roger is the central motif, and you can make your own flag from a large square of black fabric and some white poster paint.

To transform a climbing frame, treehouse or shed into a buccaneering pirate galleon, deck it with bunting, a few 'Keep Out' or 'Beware, Pirates!' signs, a Jolly Roger or two and lots of balloons. You could also attach a large sheet or tablecloth painted to look like a sail that's been patched up after a battle on the high seas! To create the sea, flatten out cardboard boxes and cut them into rolling waves with a craft knife or strong scissors, then paint with cheap emulsion paint. To make the waves stand up, lean them against the sides of your ship or tape cardboard offcuts onto the back to create stands.

If the party is to be held indoors, hint at life on the high seas by dressing the room with sheets of lining paper, onto which you can paint a seascape of waves and ships. Remember, too, that flags, bunting and balloons look just as much fun indoors as out.

OPPOSITE PAGE, ABOVE LEFT This rascally pirate is wearing his own stripy top teamed with a waistcoat and scarlet trousers from a bought costume.

OPPOSITE PAGE, ABOVE RIGHT An old toy trunk plays the part of a treasure chest and can be used as a dramatic-looking prop or to hold the prizes for the party games

OPPOSITE PAGE, BELOW RIGHT A home-made pirate costume looks just as good as anything you might buy, yet it's just an old white shirt and cut-off jeans teamed with a spotty scarf belt and a waistcoat.

OPPOSITE PAGE, BELOW LEFT, AND THIS PAGE Silly accessories will go down a storm. Put together a box of plastic hooks and eye patches so that arriving pirates can embellish their costumes.

Just as the Jolly Roger alerts anyone to the presence of pirates, an eye patch, headscarf and a stripy top or big white shirt are all that a child will need to play the part of a pirate. Charity shops are a great source of clothes that can be customized to create a pirate outfit. Old jeans cut in bold zigzags just below the knee look great – just add a white shirt with some patches sewn on here and there, a waistcoat and a headscarf, and you have a salty shipwrecked sea dog!

If your child's guests are slow to warm up, or don't know one another, a treasure chest filled with fun accessories such as eye patches, money pouches containing 'pieces of eight' and false beards can work as an ice-breaker. Place it in the centre of the room and, as you introduce each pirate to the rest, let them choose a prop to add to their costumes.

Decorating pirate hats is lots of fun, and also makes a good party activity. Get everything ready beforehand and make sure that you have more than enough for the number of children invited – someone is bound to feel dissatisfied with their creation and want to start all over again. The pirate hats shown here are made from two pieces of black card or strong paper. One piece is a strip that is used to form a headband around the child's head, and the other is a simple hat shape to stick to the front of the headband. Equip the children with some white poster paint and brushes and some images of skulls and crossbones to copy, and they will be kept busy and happy for half an hour.

A treasure hunt is another fun pirate-themed activity that any group of little pirates will enjoy. Bear in mind that the clues need to be very simple for this age group, and it would probably work best if a parent helped by leading the pirates through the clues to find the buried treasure.

ABOVE LEFT The ship's wheel was hired from a party shop, but you can make your own from cardboard or get your children to improvise with an old wheel.

BELOW LEFT Give each child a treasure map as part of a game, then send them off to hunt for individual prizes or to embark on a group treasure hunt. To make your maps more authentic, age the paper by soaking it in strong tea.

ABOVE AND OPPOSITE PAGE Team a stripy T-shirt with a waistcoat and a headscarf for instant pirate attire. Add an eye patch and plastic hook for added fun!

adventure on the high seas

Organize a fun assault course for your pirates. Establish two 'islands', one at each end of the garden, and arrange a chain of chairs, cushions, a plank of wood raised on bricks and so on across the garden. Tell the children that the grass is a shark-infested ocean, and that their goal is to get across without falling in – the winner is the one who completes the task fastest.

party plan

By their third birthday, children really appreciate a party, and by the age of four they will not only expect a party, but will also have strong views about what it should entail. Most three- and four-year-olds will arrive accompanied by at least one parent and perhaps a sibling or two, whereas most five-year-olds are happy to be left to fend for themselves, which makes numbers more manageable.

WHERE SHALL WE HAVE IT?

• Your choice of venue will be dependent on the number of guests. Entertaining a large group of children while also providing for their parents and siblings can feel like a tall order, and also requires a fair amount of space.

• Think about numbers: parties for this age group tend to work best if they are kept small – six to eight kids in total.

• If your home is big enough, then this is the obvious choice: it doesn't involve hire costs, it doesn't matter what the weather is like, there is a toilet at hand, and food won't need to be transported.

• If numbers mean that home is out of the question, or if you can't face the mess, try a local community centre or church hall.

• For summer birthdays, a local park is a good alternative. Most games can be transposed to the park, and children enjoy picnics.

WHAT'S THE BEST TIME?

• The best times are either 11am–1.30pm, when you can provide games and lunch, or 3–5pm, when you can provide a birthday tea.

WHAT FOOD SHOULD WE SERVE?

• Keep it simple: cookie-cutter sandwiches (see page 114), veggie sticks and cherry tomatoes. Sausages on sticks and pineapple chunks with cheese are also fun and easy. Don't offer too much choice, and start with savoury foods before producing sweet treats.

• For an outdoor party, a picnic served in cardboard lunchboxes works well. A sandwich, a bag of popcorn, a carton of juice and a chocolate crispie cake is plenty. If transporting a cake is too complicated, a pile of fairy cakes makes a great replacement – simply stick candles on the top.

PRIZES AND PARTY BAGS

• For parties near any national festival, theme the treats accordingly. At Christmas, packs of paper-chain strips are good, or a small tree ornament along with a personalized cookie, while at Halloween a plastic spider and a ghoulish mask would be ideal.

• Three- and four-year-olds are more than happy to walk off with a large cookie or gingerbread figure (see page 128), especially if it bears their initial and is prettily wrapped. Add a balloon as a bonus.

• If guests are slow to leave, party bags will come into their own – hand them over only as your guests leave, and you'll be guaranteed an empty house in no time!

• Bubbles may seem like a good, cheap party-bag treat, but most parents loathe them – small children more often than not end up tipping the liquid all over the car on the way home.

• A word on prizes: if you want the children to eat the food you have prepared, avoid giving sweets as prizes before the meal. Instead, hand out stickers. Give a sheet of them to the winner and single stickers to other players to keep everyone happy.

GAMES AND ACTIVITIES

Third birthdays

• Keep games simple and avoid long instructions. A simple treasure hunt searching for chocolate coins or small plastic animals will be a great hit (don't be too ingenious with your hiding places, though).

• Musical Bumps (see page 102) is good for this age.

• Three-year-olds will want to play most games several times, so a treasure hunt and Musical Bumps can easily fill the run-up to tea.

• For an outdoor party, a ball is all you'll need. Provide an adult- and child-friendly picnic and everyone will have a good time.

Fourth birthdays

• Pass the Parcel (see page 103) is a favourite, but you may need to assist. Doughnut Eating or the simple version of The Chocolate Game (see page 104) are lots of fun for both children and parents.

• If you live near a park, try a bikes and trikes party. Arrange for everyone to gather at an easily identifiable spot in the park. Plan a route from this point to the picnic spot (keep it short – they can always do it twice) and, once everyone has arrived, the children can set off en masse, with parents directing operations and keeping tabs on stragglers. This sort of outdoor party is not as dependent upon good weather – a drizzly bike ride is just as much fun as a sunny one, just as long as you have a sheltered spot for your picnic.

Fifth birthdays

• All of the above will work, as will Pin the Tail on the Donkey (see page 103), although some children may not want to be blindfolded.

• Musical Statues and Sleeping Lions (see page 102) are also ideal for this age.

OPPOSITE PAGE Cowboys and cowgirls eat at a table made from bales of hay (available from stables or pet shops). The cacti were made from painted cardboard and reinforced with bamboo poles.

LEFT This Indian chief's headdress was shop-bought, but coloured feathers are also available from craft shops.

RIGHT A real campfire may be out of the question, but faking one is easy. Pile sticks together, then make flames from red and yellow tissue paper.

BELOW A cowboy laundry bag is used to store prizes.

A Wild West party has something for everyone. The costumes are easy (who doesn't have a pair of jeans?). So is the food – burgers, hot dogs and corn on the cob.

wild west

Evoking the spirit of the Wild West in an urban back garden is surprisingly easy and can involve very little in the way of decorations; just a bale or two of hay (available from pet shops or local stables), a length of gingham and some cacti cut from flattened-out cardboard boxes.

If you have the time and the inclination, add a log cabin, made from cardboard painted to look like wood, and a fake campfire made from real twigs set ablaze with tissue paper flames. Or you could really go to town, taking your cue from those behind-the-scenes photographs of Hollywood westerns, where the archetypal one-horse town comprising a bar, a jail and a few other buildings is revealed to be just a series of stage flats. You can create your own Wild West scenery at home with cardboard boxes and some tins of cheap paint. First, flatten out the boxes and then cut them up or stick them together with strong packing tape to create the shapes that you want. Next, paint on the details, keeping the look bold and simple, rather like a cartoon. To secure your scenery, tape bamboo garden canes to the back of each 'building' and drive them into the ground like windbreakers on a beach. If the party is being held indoors, it's even easier to simply paint a bold frontier town on a sheet of cheap lining paper.

A child's playhouse can easily be adapted to fit the theme – simply attach a sign saying 'Sheriff' or 'Saloon' or tack some gingham curtains to the windows to create a frontier homestead. An Indian tipi can be improvised from bamboo poles draped with dustsheets or a tablecloth.

The costumes for a Wild West party couldn't be easier to put together. For boys and girls alike, a pair of jeans, a checked or denim shirt and a cowboy hat are all it takes to become a cool cowhand. For something a little more sophisticated, patches of gingham or suede sewn onto ordinary denim shirts will give them a western spin. Charity shops are a great source of cheap tops to customize – look out for fake or real suede or leather clothes, which can be cut up to create chaps, waistcoats and tunics.

Cowboys are not the only fancy dress option for a party with a western theme. Girly girls who resist jeans at all costs could go as showgirls from the local saloon – a much more glamorous possibility!

ABOVE An old fake suede skirt found in a charity shop was cut up to create the fringing on this denim shirt. The cowgirl in the background is wearing a simple white shirt, onto which gingham and white fringing has been sewn. This sort of adaptation is quickly done using a machine. If you have pinking shears, you won't need to worry about hemming edges, either.

LEFT Joke-shop accessories, such as this plastic arrow or pop-guns with flags saying 'BANG!', are perfect accessories.

OPPOSITE PAGE A play-house adds to the fun.

Dress them up in velvet dresses, lace trims and feathers to wear in their hair. For law-abiding boys, sheriffs' outfits are just a matter of adding shiny badges and waistcoats. And then there are the Native American chiefs and squaws, perhaps the most dramatic costumes of them all. Simple squaw tunics can be made from old dustsheets or lengths of fake suede – cut the hems to create a fringed effect and sew on some strips of contrasting trim to look like embroidery. Indian chief headdresses are available for hire or to buy in party shops, but are easy to cobble together if you buy a pack of feathers from a craft shop or specialist craft catalogue.

The more over-the-top the props and scenery for this party, the more the children will love them. And cardboard (as long as it's not left out in the rain) is surprisingly durable. So don't throw away your handiwork – your kids will enjoy the cacti, saloon bar and jail for a long time after the party has ended.

LEFT Make headdresses using strips of bright fabric or furniture trimmings and add colourful feathers. Face paints complete the look.

BELOW LEFT Swinging bar doors cut from cardboard look fantastic attached to the deck and turn it into a western saloon.

RIGHT These giant cacti were made from large packing cases flattened out, cut to shape and painted. Extra-long garden canes are attached to the back both to support the cacti and stake them into the ground.

OPPOSITE PAGE A colourful tipi bought from a mail-order catalogue complements the sheriff's playhouse and neatly creates two camps.

make it a wild, wild party A Wild West theme is perfect for a party with lots of energetic races and team games. You can pitch squaws against braves, and sheriffs against rustlers, or revive that old classic and set cowboys against Indians!

From the sequin-spangled glamour of the trapeze artist to the red-nosed silliness of the clown, a circus party gives children a wonderful opportunity to dive into the dressing-up box and use their imaginations.

circus

There is no doubt about it: transforming your room into a big top will involve a bit of effort, but it's well worth it. After all, what is a circus without its tent?

Tenting a room is pretty simple, and doesn't involve any sewing, but it will require lots of fabric and a bit of fiddling about with staples and string. Although you can guess at how much fabric you will need, it's worth taking the time to measure up properly. The best way to work out how much fabric you'll need is to attach one end of a ball of string to the ceiling where the centre of your big top will be.

Unreel the string out towards the wall, allowing it to slacken to form a gentle curve, and attach it here with sticky tape before dropping the ball to the floor. Cut the string just past the point where it meets the floor, and then take it down and measure its length. This is how much fabric you'll need for one stripe of the tent, so multiply this length by however many stripes you plan to put up. Go for the lightest, cheapest and brightest fabric you can find.

Once you have bought your fabric (ask the shop to cut it into the lengths you require), place all the

OPPOSITE PAGE, FAR LEFT, AND THIS PAGE A toy basket filled with traditional silly jokes is a great ice-breaker. Let the children dive in and enjoy mucking about.

OPPOSITE PAGE, ABOVE RIGHT A sparkly top hat bought from a party shop completes a home-made ringmaster's outfit. The costume comprises a ballet leotard and a sequinned dress from a charity shop, which was cut up to create a waistcoat and matching wristbands.

OPPOSITE PAGE, BELOW RIGHT This adorable little lion's mane was made from an oval piece of fake fur, which had a hole cut out of the centre and was then sewn onto a plastic hairband. Face paints were used to create the nose and whiskers.

lengths together and tie them together at one end with a piece of string. This is the centre of your big top. Attach the bunched-together ends to the centre of your ceiling. Next, take one of the fabric panels and draw it out towards the point where the walls meet the ceiling. Allow the panel enough slack, so it falls in a loose swag, then attach the fabric to the wall with staples or tacks. Let the end fall loose to the floor. Repeat this process until you have created your very own big top!

If you have any fabric left over, use it to cover the tea table, or to create an awning over a buffet-style food stall. Pile bright plastic bowls with popcorn and let children eat it from paper cones. Choose paper plates and cups in gaudy fairground colours or decorated with stripes that recall the big top.

Even if they've never been to one, children know that the circus means clowns, high-wire acts and a top-hatted ringmaster. They'll also know that circuses traditionally included animals such as big cats, sea lions and elephants, all of which give lots of scope for costumes. Although professionally made versions

OPPOSITE PAGE Children will enjoy choosing from a buffet tea, especially if it's set out to look like a fairground stall. Cut lengths of cheap red and yellow muslin into strips, and hem by folding the edges and securing them with double-sided tape.

LEFT Let guests take it in turns to be the strong man! Take a large sheet of cardboard and paint your figure with poster paints.

ABOVE RIGHT Serve popcorn in home-made paper cones – just roll up a sheet of paper and secure with sticky tape.

BELOW Decorate shop-bought gingerbread characters to fit the theme, or make your own (see recipe on page 129).

roll up, roll up, and have your face painted! A decent set of face paints is a really sound investment, even if you are not particularly skilled at applying them. Children love being made up to look like their favourite characters, and they won't mind about wobbly lines as long as the colours are vibrant and the details are bold.

ABOVE LEFT AND CENTRE Set up a face-painting stand and decorate the children's faces to match their costumes. This will be very popular, so you may wish to enlist the help of another parent.

LEFT AND ABOVE RIGHT This trapeze artist sports a sparkly leotard and a feather boa worn as a tutu, teamed with a pair of sequinned pumps onto which silk ribbons were sewn. The metallic mask came from a party shop.

of all these characters are readily available, making your own costumes is very straightforward and can be fun, too!

A clown costume can be created from a pair of oversized stripy pyjama bottoms, braces, a bright T-shirt and a pair of Dad's shoes. A big red nose is the finishing touch. A trapeze artist needs a leotard, sparkly tights and a feathered mask. Animals are just as easy. Look for basic clothes such as leggings, tights and T-shirts in the right colours (brown, yellow, black or orange, depending on the animal), and then concentrate on defining details, such as large cardboard ears for an elephant, a wild fluffy mane for a lion or stripy facial markings for a tiger.

Children in fancy dress always enjoy each other's costumes. Put on some marching music and organize a circus parade at the start of the party. Award small prizes for their efforts, and make sure everyone wins a prize for some aspect of their costume.

THIS PICTURE, AND ABOVE AND BELOW RIGHT This clown looks fantastic, with his big red nose, mismatched stripy suit and big feet. Only his hat, nose and shoes were bought for the party; the rest of his costume was home-made. The jacket was customized with bright braid and funny buttons. His large red mouth and silly eyebrows were painted on with face paints and make him really look the part. You don't have to be particularly skilled with face paints to create fun transformations. Once you have covered a child's face with a base colour such as white, pink or yellow, you can then build up simple details. Here (right and above right) the children just wanted fun motifs such as butterflies, hearts and beauty spots.

OPPOSITE PAGE A cardboard rocket that came as a flat-pack kit has been embellished with silver foil and details cut from sheets of wrapping paper. This forms the centrepiece of the lunar landscape room. The rocket girl's no-sew outfit was made from foam camping mats.

LEFT The blue star mats on the floor were cut from camping mats so the kids could kneel comfortably round the low tea table.

RIGHT Rubber finger-top monsters make great prizes or treats for the goody bags.

BELOW CENTRE Details on the rocket girl's outfit were simply glued on.

BELOW RIGHT Water pistols double up as excellent ray guns!

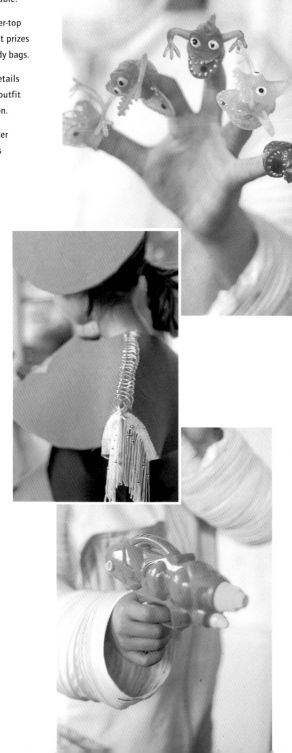

As your house fills up with aliens and astronauts, it will feel like a space station at the end of the universe. Decorative stars and planets complete the atmosphere.

space

The style of decorations you choose for a space party will depend on how much time you have, and whether or not you enjoy playing around with egg-boxes, tin foil, cardboard and silver spray!

Decking the house with silver stars and a planet or two is quick and easy. Cut stars of different sizes from pieces of cardboard or flattened packing cases. Cover them with tin foil, attach a length of cotton and hang the stars from the ceiling or in the windows. Planets can be made in exactly the same way. Alternatively, buy a few cheap paper globe lampshades in different sizes and paint them to resemble the moon and some of the more colourful planets.

A rocket makes a very effective centrepiece for a space party – it has a real wow factor and is not difficult to make. Flat-pack playhouse rockets are available from mail-order catalogues, or you can make your own from several large cardboard boxes taped together. Ask for a couple of large packing cases (such as the sort used for transporting fridges or washing machines) at your local department store. Use the tallest box to create the central section of your rocket, and attach a smaller box, cut, folded and taped to create a pointed nose cone.

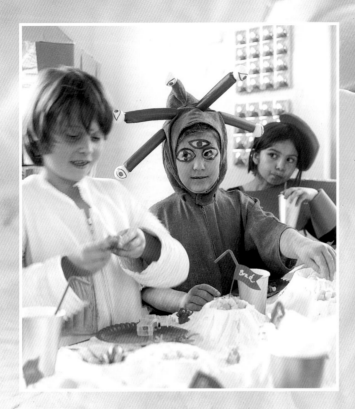

If you're feeling creative, take the space theme one step further with a lunar tea table. Although it looks complicated, it takes just twenty minutes to make and it's something that your children will really enjoy helping you with. However, it is an extremely messy process, so make sure you cover the floor with a dustsheet or, better still, make it in the garden.

You will need several plastic flower pots with their bottoms sawn off, and a sheet of MDF or chipboard that is a similar size to the table on which it will sit. Glue the flower pots to the board, widest sides down, then drape a large sheet of muslin over the whole table top. The sheet needs to be large enough to hang over the edge of the table and also to hang down into the flower pots. In a bucket, mix up a packet of powdered filler (such as Polyfilla) with enough water to make a thick yet pourable mixture, like thick double cream.

Now for the fun bit! Using your hands or a big paintbrush, slap the mixture roughly all over the muslin. The lunar craters will form as the weight of the mixture weighs the muslin down in the flower pots. Although the mixture sets quickly it needs to dry for at least half a day, so don't try to move it immediately.

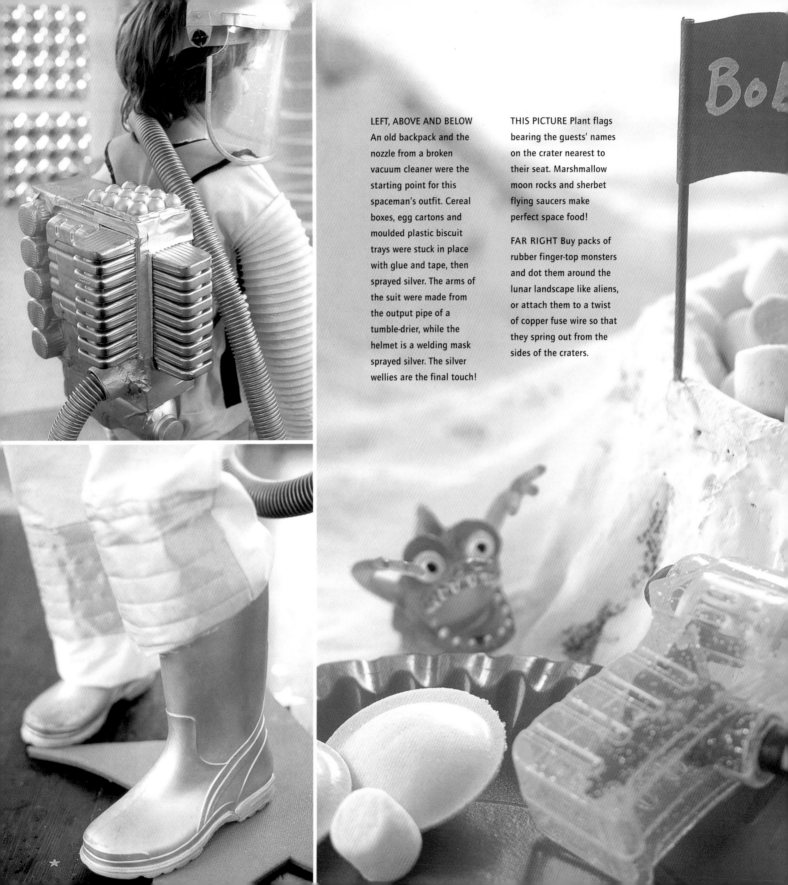

LEFT, ABOVE AND BELOW
An old backpack and the nozzle from a broken vacuum cleaner were the starting point for this spaceman's outfit. Cereal boxes, egg cartons and moulded plastic biscuit trays were stuck in place with glue and tape, then sprayed silver. The arms of the suit were made from the output pipe of a tumble-drier, while the helmet is a welding mask sprayed silver. The silver wellies are the final touch!

THIS PICTURE Plant flags bearing the guests' names on the crater nearest to their seat. Marshmallow moon rocks and sherbet flying saucers make perfect space food!

FAR RIGHT Buy packs of rubber finger-top monsters and dot them around the lunar landscape like aliens, or attach them to a twist of copper fuse wire so that they spring out from the sides of the craters.

Bob

lost property Children tend to shed bits of their costumes during the course of a party. Set aside a box for abandoned ray guns and visors, and the children can retrieve their stuff at home time.

If messing about with powdered filler doesn't appeal, don't worry. The costumes for this party are easy to make, and they look so good that they will create much of the atmosphere. Our spaceman's fabulous silvery jet-pack was constructed from an old backpack, onto which were glued various plastic trays from chocolate boxes and parts from a broken vacuum cleaner, before the whole thing was sprayed silver. On his arms, the spaceman is wearing an old ventilation tube from a tumble-drier.

The cute rocket girl costume was made from cheap foam camping mats that were cut into large circles to create a skirt, breastplate and hat. The pieces for the skirt and breastplate had holes cut in the centre for the child to wriggle into, while the cuffs were offcuts that were shaped and secured using ribbon ties that were knotted into place. The fringed detailing was glued on at the end.

FAR LEFT Create stained-glass windows by sticking coloured cellophane to the windowpanes. Add heraldic shields cut from thin silver card to make it look more dramatic.

LEFT This hat was hired, but a similar one could be made from scraps of fabric and a cone of rolled card.

The flags and banners that feature so heavily in images of medieval jousts were the inspiration for this party. Bold and simple, these decorations are great fun to make, and your kids will enjoy helping you conjure up a medieval tournament.

knights and princesses

This party theme is unusual in that it's hugely appealing to both boys and girls, which makes it a great option for this age group. By the age of six (and often even younger), children have strong views about whether or not certain toys, games and colours are appropriate for their gender. This can make some fancy dress themes problematic. Some girls may dismiss anything and everything to do with space and the Wild West, for instance, because they regard them as boyish. Similarly, boys may feel that the circus is slightly girly.

Bold knights and beautiful princesses, however, present no such problems. Once in their helmets, plastic swords in hand, the boys won't care that the other half of the party guests are swishing around in floaty pink dresses and pointy hats with veils – and vice versa.

In terms of decorations, this is a particularly fun theme to work on with your children. The decorative details are very easy to make, and involve nothing more than cutting and glueing. Once you have chosen their design, banners and flags can be made as if on a production line.

OPPOSITE PAGE Banners hung from bamboo canes and lengths of wrapping paper cut into pennants and taped along the bookcase are all it takes to create a chamber fit for a king and queen! The decorations look amazing but were easy to make.

The hanging banners were made by sticking two sheets of A2 paper together along their short sides and embellishing them with shapes cut from paper in contrasting colours. The key is to keep the details simple – bold shapes such as shields, squares and circles work best. A pair of pointed tails (large triangles of paper) stuck to the bottom edge completes each banner. Thick craft paper is ideal for making these banners – bumper-sized packs are widely available from both specialist art outlets and most good toy shops.

As with the other themes, scour the house for suitable props. Here, an antique chair was transformed into the party girl's throne, while two garden tealight holders were fashioned into medieval sconces, their tops filled with flames made from scrunched-up paper and cellophane.

Other props, such as swords and shields, are easy to make from cardboard and silver paper. Or, if you want something more robust, plastic versions are available from party shops – as are helmets.

OPPOSITE PAGE Even home-made headgear looks very professional if you use richly textured fabrics, shiny paper, plastic gems and fake fur trim to decorate it.

BELOW LEFT This helmet was made from papier mâché. To make something similar, find a mould close in size to your child's head, such as a plastic bowl or blown-up balloon. Cover it with petroleum jelly then layer on the papier mâché. When dry, paint silver and finish with several layers of varnish for extra protection.

BELOW Make Musical Bumps more regal, with velvet cushions to land on!

ABOVE RIGHT Toy knights are great for marking the children's places for tea.

To make your own suit of armour, all you need is a cardboard box, a ball of string and some spray-on silver paint. Cut two oblongs from the box to create a front and back breastplate. Next, cut two strips of card about 5–10 cm wide and long enough to curve over each shoulder from front to back. Make holes at either end of these strips and then make holes in the top corners of your two breastplates. With strong string, tie the strips into place to create a 'sandwich board' suit of armour, which can then be sprayed silver to resemble armour. Finally, make a hole halfway down on either side of each panel, and thread a length of string through in order to attach the armour more firmly to its wearer.

Costumes for the princesses are very easy. A favourite party dress topped with a tall pointed hat is pretty much all that's needed, or perhaps a crown sitting on top of a diaphanous veil. To make a pointed hat, take a large piece of lightweight card and twist to form a cone. Secure with sticky tape and staples, then cover with pretty fabric or wrapping paper. Attach a long ribbon, a pretty scarf or a length of coloured muslin to the top, to create a veil.

LEFT The party princess sits in state on her throne to receive her guests.

ABOVE The sconces on either side of the throne were from a garden centre and are designed to hold large tealights in the garden. Here, they have been filled with scrunched-up sheets of yellow and red tissue paper and cellophane to create pretend flames.

OPPOSITE PAGE, ABOVE CENTRE This pointed hat is covered with brocade.

OPPOSITE PAGE, ABOVE RIGHT A valiant sentry stands guard holding his burning sconce.

OPPOSITE PAGE, BELOW LEFT AND RIGHT A professionally made costume is a worthwhile investment if your child often plays games based around this theme.

a knight's quest A forfeit game is ideal for a knights and princesses party. Write out a selection of simple 'quests' on pieces of paper, then fold them and put them in a bowl. Ask the children to pick out a forfeit, and award them a sticker if they complete it. The child with the most stickers wins.

party plan

By the age of six, party invitees will be dropped off by their parents and you will be left in sole charge. If your child's whole class is invited, you may need to draft in a few other mothers to help out.

WHERE SHALL WE HAVE IT?
• This will depend on the type of party you decide to have – how many guests and what you plan to do.
• At this age children will have a clear idea about who they wish to invite to their party, so you may end up either with fewer children than in previous years, or many more, and this will be the deciding factor for the location.
• Ask yourself if your house can really take thirty seven-year-olds – would a local school hall or community centre be better?
• For a sports-day party or other outdoor activities, you can stay at home if your garden can take it, or relocate to the local park for the afternoon.

WHAT'S THE BEST TIME?
• Work around what suits you best. Do you want to hold the party straight after school from 4 to 6pm? Or would you prefer to do it at the weekend, when you can base it around lunch, tea or supper?
• If your child is prone to getting overexcited, a lunchtime party is a good idea as they won't have to suppress their hysteria for quite so long!

WHAT FOOD SHOULD WE SERVE?
• For a party straight after school, give the children a drink and a snack when they arrive, as they'll be ravenous. A packet of crisps or a piece of fruit is all they'll need before getting down to the games.

• For the party tea, plan the food to suit the theme and location. A party in the park is best done as a picnic, or with individual picnic boxes containing sandwiches, fruit, crisps and an iced fairy cake.
• For a party straight after school, base the birthday tea around a favourite week-night meal – bangers and mash, for example, or spaghetti Bolognese followed by jelly and ice cream for pudding. Feel no guilt if your child demands fish fingers and chips!
• Do the cake and candles routine just before the children depart, then add a slice of cake to each going-home present.

PRIZES AND PARTY BAGS
• If the party is themed, try matching the presents to the theme, as the children are now old enough to appreciate the effort.
• Toffee apples are great goodbye presents for both cowboy and circus parties; perfect, too, for a Halloween bash. For spacemen, attach streamers so that they look like meteors with fiery tails.
• Mini cacti wrapped in cellophane and tied with a tag bearing each child's name are all you need for a western-themed party, though you could expand on this with any cowboy-related bits and pieces such as rubbers, stickers and so on that you find.
• Plastic swords are cheap and perfect to send knights off with, while big plastic rings and girly trinkets such as hair accessories, hand mirrors or make-up will send princesses home happy.
• A circus party bag could contain either brightly coloured treats such as rubbers and pens in circus colours, or a selection of joke-shop classics, such as flowers that squirt water.
• Rocket or star stickers, inflatable globes and alien pen-toppers are all perfect for a space-related party.

• Whoopee cushions or other silly jokes are guaranteed to raise a laugh from all age groups, while rubber insects or bouncy balls seem to have an enduring appeal for little boys.

GAMES AND ACTIVITIES

• There is almost no limit to the games you can play with this age group. Almost all the games featured on pages 102–107 can be adapted to suit children of six and up.

• Pass the Parcel with forfeits between the layers (see page 103) is a great ice-breaker, as are Musical Chairs, Bumps and Statues (see page 102). They are also good for burning off a bit of excess energy at the start of the party or before teatime.

• A themed Pin the Tail on the Donkey (see page 103) with either a dragon, alien or circus animal is a fun classic that all children know how to play.

• Include a couple of no-prize games, too, such as What's the Time Mr Wolf? (see page 106), which children are sure to want to play several times.

• If your party is based on the idea of a sports day, limit yourself to classic races (see page 107) with a few other activities, such as Apple Bobbing and Doughnut Eating thrown in, so that less sporty guests still have a chance to do well in something.

• If your party is being held at home and space is tight, limit the games to those that can be played around the table-top, such as Kim's Game (see page 105) or the Flour Game (see page 104).

• For smaller groups, an activity-based party will keep guests both entertained and contained: try decorating pots, T-shirts or masks. This can all be done sitting around a table with a selection of paints, glue and decorations in the centre. You will need to forewarn parents or provide overalls, so children don't ruin their best clothes.

LEFT AND RIGHT Colourful decorations set the theme for this party. Bold tropical flowers (right) can be made from colourful tissue paper. Cut out two pieces of paper in a figure-of-eight shape and place them on top of each other in the shape of a cross. Take a pipe cleaner and bend it in two to make the stamen. Stick the pipe cleaner through the centre of the flower and secure with sticky tape.

Create a tropical paradise whatever the weather, with funky decorations in hot pinks, lush greens and vivid blues. Guests should wear their loudest shirts and largest shades, or grass skirts and flower garlands.

tropical island

Hula girls, Hawaiian shirts, flower garlands and drinks with silly names are the key ingredients for a party with a tropical theme. If the time of year is right, and your garden is lush enough, then tables teamed with straw parasols will set the mood. Although these are now available from most DIY outlets and garden centres, you can easily adapt your own garden parasol with layers of fringed tissue paper.

Tablecloths in zingy yellows and greens add to the tropical mood, as do bright flower garlands strung around the party area (if the party is indoors,

arrange them in swags along shelves, across windows and over the fireplace).

Many of the paper decorations in these pictures are available from party shops or the party sections of supermarkets. But, to create the look yourself, you will need scissors, glue, pipe cleaners and lots of bright tissue paper. The tropical flowers are made from two sheets of paper cut into a figure-of-eight shape, then placed on top of one another at right angles. The stamens are made by bending two red or yellow pipe cleaners in half, curling over the ends and inserting them in the centre of the tissue paper

OPPOSITE PAGE Conjure up a lush tropical paradise with garden furniture that has been dressed to look the part. The tropical sunshades came from a DIY store and the paper flowers and garlands are a mixture of shop-bought and home-made items.

flowers. Finally twist the middle of the tissue paper around the bent ends of the pipe cleaners, secure with sticky tape, open out the petals, and you have an exotic bloom. Arrange the flowers in groups or string them from threads to form garlands.

If the party is taking place in the evening, think about lighting. As long as there is adult supervision, older children are safe around floating tealights bobbing in bowls of water, and floral versions especially make wonderful tropical table decorations. Fairy lights are available in many designs these days – look for strings of flowers or strands of twinkling multicoloured lights. Other details that children will love include fun cocktail accessories, such as tiny paper parasols, little plastic monkeys and paper palm trees. Buy packs of novelty plastic ice cubes, too, and fill a bucket with them. Set up a bar from which food and drinks will be served, and arrange pitchers of tropical punch (see page 125), pineapple juice and other exotic juices, which the children can mix as they wish.

OPPOSITE PAGE Dress up drinks with paper parasols and other kitsch accessories. Set up a bar serving fruity 'mocktails' made from mango and pineapple juice, or place jugs of tropical juices on the tables so the guests can help themselves.

THIS PAGE Flower-shaped tealights floating in bowls of water are pretty table decorations. Dress chairs with flower garlands that the children can pick up and add to their own costumes. If you are organizing a team event such as a quiz, you could use the garlands to denote teams – pink for one, blue for another, for example.

RIGHT A colourful parrot decoration adds a truly tropical touch to the 'straw' parasols!

INSET Sunglasses and garlands, handed out as the guests arrive, get everyone in the mood, as do the exotic 'mocktails' served in huge glasses with fun accessories.

OPPOSITE PAGE, ABOVE RIGHT Brightly coloured sweets look like decorations in their own right.

OPPOSITE PAGE, BELOW RIGHT Pretty paper lanterns look as good during the day as they do when lit at night. Hang them around tables, from trees, and to decorate the 'bar' area.

all grown up At this age children really enjoy the chance to behave like little adults, so you may find that, as long as there is some music playing, the guests will want to spend some time chatting and admiring each other's costumes. One or two events such as a quiz and a limbo competition, either side of the food, are all you will need in the way of entertainment.

For the costumes, children just need to hunt out the most colourful or floral items in their wardrobes, and then acccessorize with outsize sunglasses and flower garlands. It's a nice idea to greet each guest by presenting them with a flower garland, or cheap sunglasses (or these could be sent out with the invitations to set the tone for the party). Boys can wear their swimming shorts or surf shorts with a loose shirt or colourful T-shirt. For girls, look for grass skirts in party or costume shops, or make one yourself from layers of shredded crêpe paper.

If your child likes the idea of this party but his or her birthday is in the dead of winter, it's easy to adapt the theme by taking it indoors, cranking up the central heating for the evening and having a Hawaiian disco. Track down kitsch hula music on the internet or from a big music store. Once the children have admired one another's outfits, kick off the evening's fun with a lively limbo-dancing competition. Children will find this really funny and it could also be repeated again towards the end of the party. If you have enough room to arrange the children into small groups, a quiz is a great mid-party activity for this age group, and the perfect way to calm things down after the frenzied exertions of the limbo dancing or before the food is served!

OPPOSITE PAGE Children love the sophistication of costumes that feel like 'real' glamorous grown-up clothes. These costumes are a mixture of bought, hired and home-made clothes and accessories.

RIGHT The 'cocktail bar' is made from a narrow trestle table concealed with lining paper. The Deco-style decorations were cut from paper and glued in place. A starched white tablecloth would look just as good.

As a child, one of the joys of dressing up is getting your hands on your parents' clothes, and this party caters for that perfectly! Children love the glamour and sophistication of the theme; they also adore the grown-up feel of the costumes and accessories.

gangsters and molls

If you are prepared to do a little basic sewing, you can create outfits for this theme that will not only survive the party, but will live on in the dressing-up box long afterwards. All the accessories, such as long bead necklaces, felt trilby-style hats, feather boas and long gloves, can be picked up cheaply and easily from party shops or charity shops, as can the boys' suits and girls' dresses. However, making a costume yourself is more satisfying and often cheaper.

Flapper-style dresses are very easy to make, if you use a nylon slip with spaghetti straps or a nightdress as a base. Onto this, sew lengths of long silky fringing or a few petal-shaped panels of light silky fabric to create a fluttering layered skirt. Making the pretty headbands couldn't be simpler – invest in a pack of cheap stretchy nylon hairbands from the chemist, and sew on fabric flowers or flamboyant feathers to glamorous effect.

A home-made gangster outfit is also a matter of adapting and customizing clothing you may already have to hand. A discarded pair of dark trousers can become a passable, if cartoon-like, pinstripe if you have a steady hand, some white paint and a fine paintbrush! Look for men's jackets in small sizes in charity shops, and customize them in the same way. If you can't find a suitable jacket, simply opt for a waistcoat instead. Look out for ties and smart shirts. Jazz up an old hat with a ribbon hatband, or make spats from white paper.

If you have enough space, create a bar area from which the children can be served their 'mocktails', or perhaps they could even create their own. The idea of a nightclub will really appeal to nine- and ten-year-olds and it is, of course, the perfect complement to the apparent glamour and sophistication of the party's theme. If you have one, set up a trestle table with a smart tablecloth and add an

speakeasy style Glamour is the order of the day for this party, so set up a mirror in a corner and provide some bright-pink blusher and red lipstick, for the girls. Add a few fake moustaches or black and brown face paint, and you'll find that the boys will join in as well!

ice bucket, a sleek cocktail shaker and a selection of glasses and other cocktail paraphernalia to create the right ambience. Similarly, creating a 'soda fountain' buffet bar where children can create their own ice-cream sundaes and choose from a selection of toppings is something they will adore.

If you want to take the idea of the speakeasy still further, you can dress the room to look the part. You can decorate the wall behind the bar area with a dramatic two-tone cut-paper frieze depicting a 1930s city skyline. This can be made by drawing the outline of an imagined cityscape onto thick black paper.

OPPOSITE PAGE, LEFT A pretty brooch and a flamboyant feather were attached to a strip of fabric to create a glamorous headband.

OPPOSITE PAGE, RIGHT Give the table a touch of 1920s chic with place cards made by pasting silver foil to black card.

BELOW LEFT These bold posters were inspired by original 1920s artworks.

BELOW RIGHT A dapper false moustache cut from felt can be attached with eyelash glue.

THIS PICTURE Using real Martini glasses for mocktails is great fun for the children, who will love all the kitsch cocktail paraphernalia such as umbrellas and swizzle sticks.

ABOVE LEFT Put out the ingredients and let the children create their own cocktails. Provide a shaker and a selection of different glasses (ideally made of plastic) for long and short drinks.

OPPOSITE PAGE A table set up with hundreds and thousands, jellybeans, mini marshmallows and other treats for adorning ice-cream sundaes will be the highlight of the party.

Using a craft knife, cut it out and stick it on top of a large sheet of different-coloured card with spray adhesive. Smaller squares of the different-coloured paper were added to create the lit-window effect on the Art Deco skyscrapers.

Children will also enjoy making other decorations, such as posters. The ones shown here were influenced by *Vogue* covers from the 1920s and 1930s, and made using collage techniques and a restricted palette of black, red and silver. Each image was first drawn out on a sheet of black paper, and then traced. The tracing paper was then used as a template for the details, which were cut from sheets of black, silver or red paper. Once all the elements were cut out, they were glued onto the original drawing. Some of these posters can be hung in your entrance hall, so that they greet guests as they arrive, while others can be used to decorate the room you have transformed into a pre-teen speakeasy!

party plan

By the age of nine or ten, children will get as much pleasure from planning the party as they will from the day itself. They will really want to have a hand in making invitations and decorations, and planning all the games and activities.

WHERE SHALL WE HAVE IT?

• For a really over-the-top fancy dress party with themed decorations, home is best as you have plenty of time to get the decorations in place.

• If the party is going to be big (perhaps because it's your child's last year at primary school, say), a local hall may be better.

• You may prefer to treat your child and a select group of friends to a trip to the cinema or a meal in a restaurant. Children often really enjoy Chinese food, while some pizza restaurants can arrange pizza-making sessions with one of the chefs.

WHAT'S THE BEST TIME?

• If you are happy to abandon the usual lunch and teatime time slots, then early evening is a real treat for this age group.

• Sleepovers are popular at this age, and either tend to start straight after school on a Friday night (so that they have the weekend to recover) or on a Saturday, when you can start the party at 6pm rather than at the school gates!

WHAT FOOD SHOULD WE SERVE?

• This age group is less fussy and so you can have more fun preparing something that you know they will eat. Pizzas always go down well, whether shop-bought or home-made, as do hot dogs and burgers.

• If you are hosting a big party or a disco, a buffet often works well, and you don't have to worry so much about having enough chairs for everyone. Children often prefer grazing to a sit-down meal, so a buffet will suit them, as well.

PRIZES AND PARTY BAGS

• Children don't really need anything to take home after a sleepover party, though you will have a good idea of what the form is among your child's friends if he or she has already stayed over at someone else's house.

• For a girl's party bag you could include any or all of the following: inexpensive make-up, glittery hair accessories, fun jewellery, miniature perfume samples and little purses, all of which can be found easily on any high street.

• For a boy's party bag, you could include any or all or the following: a pack of cards, plastic boomerangs, novelty keyrings, glow-in-the-dark stickers, mini torches and any pocket-sized gadgets.

• For something more long-lasting, a book is a good idea. Look for the latest launch in a popular series. There are many different series aimed at this age group, and your child can bring you up to date with what the current favourites are.

• For both the gangsters and molls party and the tropical party, you could give children a cocktail glass with a recipe for a 'mocktail' and some fun cocktail accessories, or a sundae glass with a packet of sprinkles and something silly to stick on top.

• If you are having an activity party (see 'Games and activities'), the item the children make should be enough of a going-home present in itself, though it is always nice to send children home with a slice of birthday cake or a fairy cake, too.

GAMES AND ACTIVITIES

• Your children may have outgrown organized games by this stage, but they will still want the party to have a structure of some sort.

• Children love watching films with friends, and a favourite film or a blockbuster that's been newly released on video or DVD is perfect for an evening party or sleepover. Just set them up in front of the TV with popcorn and drinks, and give them a meal either before or after their film.

• Activity-based parties are great for this age group, as they can work on most things independently as long as all the equipment is provided. Equip a table with everything needed for one of the following.

• Tie-dye – ask children to bring a T-shirt to dye or provide them with one, and set up bowls of different coloured dyes. This is good for a sleepover party, as the T-shirts can dry overnight and be handed out as the children leave in the morning.

• Frame decorating – buy cheap, untreated wooden frames and give the children a selection of paints, some glitter, glue, buttons and other bits and pieces to decorate them with.

• Customizing T-shirts – as with tie-dyeing, either provide plain white T-shirts or ask the guests to bring along a T-shirt they wish to customize. Provide plenty of sew-on or iron-on patches, colourful fabric pens and paint, assorted buttons and trimmings and needles and thread.

• Painting china mugs and tiles – ceramic paints are available from craft shops, as are suitable plain cups, plates and tiles, all of which can be decorated at home and then fired in a domestic oven.

• Beading – this is particularly popular with girls, who love sitting and chatting while making necklaces, earrings and bracelets. Provide them with thread and dishes filled with pretty beads.

Home-made invitations are much more personal than shop-bought examples, and the style and design of your child's invitations can set the tone for their party.

invitations

As children rarely receive any post, a party invitation dropping through the letterbox or handed over at the school gates will make their day. Posting invites is a neat way of sidestepping any awkwardness when handing them out to a select few in the playground. It also means that you can avoid having to invite your child's entire class (unless you really want to!).

There are lots of ready-made invitations available in the shops, but they tend to be uninspiring. Home-made invitations are more personal, and can set the tone for the whole party. For fancy dress parties, for instance, the invitation can serve as inspiration for the guests – include eye patches for a pirate party, or sheriff's badges if the theme is the Wild West.

Once you start thinking about theme-related designs, such as a wacky clown face for a circus party, a silvery rocket for a space party, and so on, you will realize that the options are endless. However, before you (and your children) get too carried away, remember how many invitations you have to make, and tailor the design so that it is relatively quick and easy to replicate. Next, work out what you will need to create the design, and make sure that you have everything to hand: there is nothing more frustrating than getting started and then realizing that you've run out of glitter or glue.

The easiest cards to make are those made from a piece of card folded in half and then cut into a

cut and paste Young children find it frustrating not being able (or allowed) to use scissors, but they love glueing things together. Design a collage-style invitation that they can simply stick together and decorate with your help.

ABOVE LEFT The theme of this party is made clear with a simple collage.

ABOVE RIGHT This invitation doubles as a mobile. Cut a large circle from a sheet of stiff paper, then draw a spiral onto it with a pencil and cut along your line. Attach a length of thread and write the party details around the spiral.

LEFT A bold and rascally pirate head complete with real eye patch is a great idea for an invitation to a pirate party.

shape that relates to the theme of the party. Decorate the invitations with paint, glitter or collage. Cut discs of silver foil to make fish scales, or use strips of red and orange tissue paper for flames emerging from the tail of a rocket.

Other easy, yet appealing invitations for little ones are simple paper-chain designs, such as a row of teddy bears or ducks. Fold a strip of paper concertina-style, then draw the outline you wish to repeat on the front 'panel' (or use a cookie cutter as a template), and then cut around the shape. Take care not to cut through the tips of the hands or paws, which form the links of the chain. This style lends itself to many variations, such as a row of spacemen for a space-themed party, or fish for an under-the-sea theme.

Lift-the-flap cards are easy and fun. A mother hen shielding her chicks under her wing is just the thing for a farm-themed party. Take a sheet of stiff paper or thin card

THIS PAGE An elegant vintage car hints at the grown-up glamour of a gangsters and molls party. The car outline was copied from a library book and then cut out of black card, while the details, such as the car radiator, hubcaps and windows, were cut from aluminium foil and stuck in place.

THIS PAGE AND INSET ABOVE This simple duck invitation cut from folded card is echoed by the duck paper chain used as a decoration.

OPPOSITE PAGE, ABOVE RIGHT This 3D fairy pops up from a simple folded card. Her wings are cut from sparkly gift wrap, while her body is a folded triangle of card adorned with metallic star stickers.

OPPOSITE PAGE, BELOW LEFT A simple chain of teddies holding hands is just the thing for a teddy bears' picnic!

OPPOSITE PAGE, BELOW RIGHT This ice-cream sundae, made from circles of different-coloured paper glued together, looks almost good enough to eat, with its decorative sprinkling of real hundreds and thousands.

and draw and cut out a simple hen shape. Now cut out a wing shape and attach it along the top with sticky tape or glue. Under the wing, you can draw a cluster of little chicks and write down the details of the party. Invitations to any number of themed parties can be made following this principle. A castle-shaped invitation with a fold-down drawbridge would be perfect for a princesses party, while a stripy big top with a flap that opens at the centre is just the thing for a circus-themed bash.

A clever bit of prop-making will intrigue and delight older kids. For an invitation to a medieval knights and princesses party, age sheets of paper by dipping them in strong tea then creasing them. Write the party details in ink, then roll the invitation up and seal with ribbon and sealing wax. This technique can also be used to create a thrilling treasure map for a pirate party!

If you are holding a party based around team events – a sports party or a quiz – attach team colours to the cards in the form of badges, and instruct the children to wear them on the day.

Whichever approach you choose, you can be sure that, not only will your guests enjoy the novelty of the home-made invitation, but your child will also enjoy making the cards as part of the exciting build up to their party.

THIS PAGE A plastic farm animal and a first-words block book wrapped in bright paper look really charming when presented in these pretty bags with ribbons. This sort of going-home present is just right for a first or second birthday. Sets of small board books can often be picked up cheaply at remainder book stores.

RIGHT Smart sandwich boxes are useful presents and can be made to suit almost any theme. Here a few sand moulds and a bath toy make them perfect for a mermaid party.

FAR RIGHT Plastic trinket pots are a great way to present going-home treats.

BELOW RIGHT A party activity such as painting plant pots and planting up seedlings can provide the going-home present, too. Label them and hand them out at going-home time.

The party bag (or going-home present) is a nice way to say thank you to your child's guests. They can be great fun to put together and it's up to you how elaborate you want the gifts to be.

party bags

Love them or loathe them, party bags are unavoidable. For any parent organizing a child's birthday party, the issue of the going-home present can feel like one of the most contentious and stressful aspects of the whole event. Somehow, we've come to believe that the success of our child's party lies in the contents of a little plastic bag. And of course this is where the competitive parent rules supreme: tales of children being packed off home with doll's tea sets, DVDs and the latest computer games abound. It's crazy, and it doesn't have to be this way.

Think beyond those plastic bags emblazoned with cartoon characters – brown paper bags (like the ones used in takeaways) are far nicer. Bulk them out with scrunched-up tissue paper and the gifts will seem more special for having been nicely presented. The bags themselves can be decorated with potato-print patterns or glued-on sequins spelling out the children's names.

Alternatively, consider making the bag or container part of the gift itself. Beaded purses and dinky embroidered bags can be picked up cheaply in high-street fashion chains and are a present in themselves – with the addition of a few chocolate coins or some cheap make-up, no girl could

LEFT A funky flower garland coiled into a cocktail glass, a pair of shades and a parasol or swizzle stick look fabulous when wrapped in crinkly cellophane and tied with a bright ribbon.

BELOW LEFT Sports beakers filled with felt tips are a good going-home present after a sports party.

THIS PICTURE Jars of home-made playdough look charming and are perfect going-home presents for children aged three and under. Add a fun-shaped cookie cutter.

fail to be thrilled. Similarly, drawstring swimming bags are perfect for boys – add marbles, paper gliders or whatever your son is currently into.

Get into the habit of looking out for party bag items throughout the year and buying them when you see them. This means that when you realize that you've left everything till the last minute (as we all do), you'll have one or two things as a starting point. If you have daughters, save miniature perfume samples and beauty freebies, which you can pop in purses or bags as going-home treats. Look for multi-packs of toys and accessories, such as sacks of plastic animals, cars, hairclips and funky socks, which can be divided between goody bags. Children adore stickers, and bumper packs are widely available – a good way of bulking out party bags.

For really young children, keep it simple – a blown-up balloon is ideal. Helium balloons are always a winner and can be selected in shapes to match virtually any theme; tie them to slices of cake wrapped in napkins and sit them near the door, where they will look so enticing that children won't want to hang about at home time.

Home-made playdough (see page 24 for recipe) is one of the nicest going-home presents for children under five, and is easy to make. In the weeks before the party, save small jam jars or baby-food jars, soak off the labels and replace them with new ones bearing the instructions for making playdough. Experiment with vibrant colours – vivid greens, zingy pinks, hot reds and deep purples look spectacular.

If you've gone to town with the decorations for the party, give their friends one or two to take home, along with a slice of cake. Teddy bear cut-outs or giant paper flowers can be carried off to adorn your guests' bedrooms, while knights and princesses will be delighted with banners and shields. Similarly, if

ABOVE Departing spacemen will be grateful for ray guns, especially if they spray water. Add a chocolate lolly and a rubber finger-top monster. Pack goodies in little boxes rather than tacky plastic loot bags and they will be appreciated even more.

BELOW Look round the shops for party-bag goodies that tie in with the theme of your child's party. Stationery shops (as well as party shops) are often a good source of useful bits and pieces, such as these fun pirate pencil-toppers.

pretty packaging Don't think about quantity, or even about how much you spend – think instead about how to present what you are giving to your departing guests. Wrap up going-home treats nicely and you will find that even very simple things will charm the children.

ABOVE LEFT A pretty bag with a floral brooch attached is a present in itself and doesn't need to be wrapped. If you have daughters, look for little bags in the sales and snap them up for your present drawer. Similarly, bulk-buy pretty hair accessories, as they make great prizes as well as going-home treats.

ABOVE RIGHT Children's gardening equipment is widely available on the high street and a miniature water can and trowel will be very gratefully accepted.

you've made any dressing-up accessories, such as rabbit ears or pirate's eye patches, or if children have decorated items as part of the fun, they can take them home as part of their present.

Individually wrapped items, rather than bags of treats, go down well with the under-eights. Bargain bookshops are a good source of cheap storybooks, colouring books and paperbacks. A lucky dip placed by the front door is great fun for all ages and makes goodbyes easier for younger children, as they are playing one last game as they walk out of the door.

If you hate the idea of party bags, you can make the children work for their reward! As the final game at the end of the party, children of four and up could be given different-coloured bags and told to hunt for parcels wrapped in paper of the same

colour. Similarly, if you are holding a pirate party, organize a treasure hunt for chocolate coins. If you have organized an activity such as decorating plant pots, tie-dyeing T-shirts or painting tiles, then you will have a ready-made going-home treat.

Themed presents work well for most age groups. Miniature cacti in little enamel mugs are great for cowboys, while glow-in-the-dark stars are perfect for spacemen. Gingerbread biscuits, cut to any shape and decorated accordingly, are always well received. Ice them to look like princesses, teddy bears, farm animals, clowns, and so on.

As with all aspects of your child's party, if you approach going-home presents with a little imagination, what at first seemed a stressful chore can actually become a real pleasure.

THIS PAGE A stack of glossy blue boxes topped with ribbons looks so enticing that even the most reluctant child will agree to leave without fuss. Each box contains a couple of butterfly hairclips and a bottle of bubble bath nestled in a twist of pink tissue paper.

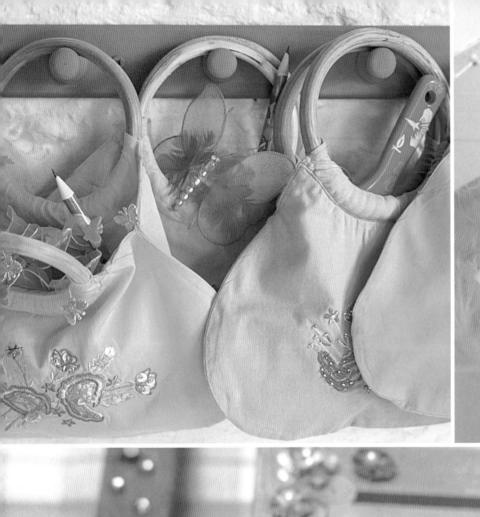

OPPOSITE PAGE, ABOVE LEFT If you have a row of children's coat pegs by the door, use them to display the going-home treats. When the time comes to leave, you'll find the children will be quick to take the hint!

OPPOSITE PAGE, BELOW Party activities are a great way to provide both entertainment and a nice memento of the party. Buy plain photo frames and let the children decorate them during the party. If you can, take a picture of each child at the party and give it to them to put in their frame when they leave.

THIS PAGE AND OPPOSITE PAGE, ABOVE RIGHT Cheap-and-cheerful presents can be given a luxurious spin if beautifully wrapped. These plastic tiaras and feather boas can be picked up for next to nothing, but look a million dollars nestling in their pretty boxes. The perfect present for little girls leaving a fairy party!

LEFT A tray of random small items collected from all around the house is all you need for half an hour's quiet entertainment playing Kim's Game (see page 105).

BELOW LEFT A hat, scarf, gloves, knife and fork and a huge bar of chocolate are laid out in preparation for the frenzied fun of the Chocolate Game (see page 104)!

RIGHT children playing Grandmother's Footsteps (see page 106) tiptoe towards their target.

OPPOSITE PAGE A lucky dip is a nice way to dole out the prizes. After each game, the winner is invited to delve into a box or bin filled with shredded paper in search of a prize. If the party is mixed, make sure that the prizes appeal to both boys and girls.

There is no denying that trying to entertain a group of overexcited children is a scary prospect. But party games are hardly rocket science and children love them, so you will be dealing with a receptive audience.

party games

When it comes to party games, lots of organization is the key to success. Ask your child which games they enjoy, what they have enjoyed playing at other parties and in the playground. Make a list of the games you have chosen. For a two-hour party, you will have time for four or five games, but it's sensible to plan for a couple extra, so if one goes wrong you can ditch it in favour of another. Next, sort out all the props and prizes that you will need. Keep your games list handy on the day, so that when the noise levels rise you can still remember what the children were meant to be doing in order to win all the prizes you've bought.

When it comes to prizes, don't set the bar too high – it's best to keep them small, and don't on any account give children a choice. Some parents hand out individual stickers or sweets (rather than whole packets) to all the players at the end of a game (or as children are eliminated), as well as giving a small prize to the winner – this is an easy but effective way of keeping everyone happy. Other parents adopt the more traditional 'winner-takes-all' approach. There is no right or wrong in this, so simply go with what you think will work best.

Sleeping Lions This is the perfect game to play when you want to calm things down. It is best for children over four, although three-year-olds will find it fun, but you will have to overlook quite a lot of twitching if the game is to last any time at all!

You need enough space for all the children to lie down comfortably.

Tell the children that they are all very, very sleepy lions and that they must lie down and remain as still as possible. Explain that if they move so much as a whisker, they will have to wake up and help you keep watch over all the other lions. Once they are all lying down, give them a moment or two to relax and stop giggling, and then you can walk among them talking to them and trying to make them laugh. Each child that is out can then help you make the others laugh, although they must not touch or tickle their 'sleeping' friends. The winner is the last child left 'sleeping'.

classic children's party games

ABOVE A blindfolded player waits eagerly to pin the tail on the donkey!

BELOW For a fairy-themed version of Musical Chairs (see right), the chairs have been replaced by home-made toadstool cushions.

Musical Chairs, Bumps and Statues These simple elimination games are great for burning off energy before tea. You will need music for all three games.

Musical Chairs Arrange as many chairs as there are children around the room. Start the music and tell the children to dance or march around the chairs. When the music stops they must find a place to sit. Once all the children are seated, you can then remove a chair, and for the next round the child with nowhere to sit is out. The game continues until there are only two players left and one chair; the winner is the child who lands on the chair first. If space is limited, replace the chairs with cushions or pieces of paper on the floor.

Musical Bumps Tell the children to keep dancing until the music stops, at which point they must sit down on the floor as quickly as they can, with a bump. The last child to sit down is out. The game continues until there is only one child left, and he or she is the winner.

Musical Statues Like Musical Bumps, all the children must dance about while the music is playing, but once it stops they must stand as still as they can until the music starts again. For young children, whose ability to stand still is limited, you will have to be lenient and make the elimination process as swift as possible.

Pass the Parcel This game can be played from three upwards, though three-year-olds are rarely happy to relinquish the parcel once it's in their sticky grasp.

You will need: a small prize wrapped in as many layers of paper as there are players, and music.

Sit all the children in a circle and hand the parcel to one of the players. Once the music starts, the parcel is passed from child to child until the music stops. At this point, the child holding the parcel can remove a layer of wrapping paper. This continues until the final layer is reached, and the child who removes this wins the prize.

Variation: Although the traditional game has only one prize, a multi-present version (including small treats between each layer of paper) has become popular.

Forfeit Pass the Parcel Older children enjoy this version, as it updates what can sometimes feel a rather babyish game. A simple forfeit or question is written on a slip of paper and placed between each layer of paper. Questions could be about films or books, while the forfeits might be singing a song or pulling a silly face. For pre-readers, insert pictures of animals and ask what noise they make.

Pin the Tail on the Donkey This is a nice quiet game, best played with the over-fours as younger children often object to being blindfolded.

You will need: a picture of a donkey or some other tailless creature, as many tails as there are children (alternatively, one tail and a marker pen to record where it was placed and by whom), a blindfold and some tape or pins to attach the tails with.

Stick the picture of the donkey to the wall at child height and mark the point where the tail should be. The child whose tail is closest to this mark will be the winner. Take each child in turn, blindfold them, give them a tail with their name on it and point them in the direction of the donkey.

Some children get bored waiting to take their turn, so it's best to sit the children on the floor to watch their friends rather than making them queue.

Variations: Kits for this game are available in party shops, but you can create your own to fit the theme of your party. Try Pin the Eyeball on the Alien for a space party, or Pin the Tail on the Charger for knights and princesses!

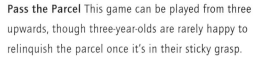

FAR LEFT AND INSET RIGHT Children enjoy messy games, which is why the flour game is especially popular. The skill of the game is to slice off just enough flour to ensure that the next player makes the mountain collapse.

LEFT The doughnut game is best played after tea, if you want them to eat any of the food you've painstakingly prepared!

RIGHT A team quiz is an excellent way to get everyone involved.

fun with food

Doughnut Eating Tie doughnuts onto lengths of string and suspend them from a washing line. Children must try to eat a whole doughnut without licking their lips. If they lick their lips, the doughnut is taken away.

The Chocolate Game Children find this game very funny, which makes it one of the most popular party games. It's also entertaining for the adults watching.

Sit the children in a circle around a plate on which there is an unwrapped bar of chocolate, a knife and fork, a hat, sunglasses, gloves and a scarf, and a die. The players roll the die until someone gets a six, at which point they quickly put on the hat, gloves, scarf and sunglasses and try to eat the bar of chocolate with the knife and fork, while the rest of the players continue rolling the die. As soon as another six is thrown, the person eating the chocolate must take everything off and the next child has a go. To make

things fairer, the children can stop throwing the die while the two players swap clothing, and then start again once the new chocolate-eater is dressed.
Variation: For younger children, stick to a hat and a pair of mittens, and a plateful of chocolate buttons, and stop play while they try to eat just one button.

The Flour Game This is a very popular game with the over fives. The Flour Game is best played at a table. On a tray, create a mini-mountain of tightly packed flour and top it with a large chunk of chocolate. The children take turns to slice away the sides of the flour mountain with a knife, taking care not to topple the chocolate. The child who eventually makes the mountain collapse has to retrieve the chocolate from the flour with their teeth. Although this can get very messy, you'll find that the children want to play this several times!

memory games and team quizzes

Team quizzes Divide the children into equally sized teams (with an even spread of children of different ages if the party includes a mix of age groups). Set them simple questions about their favourite books and films, and subjects they are working on at school. The teams can either write down their answers, or you can give each team a bell to ring or a special noise to make in place of a buzzer.

Twenty Questions, or Animal, Vegetable or Mineral Each child is given a card on which the name of an animal, a person or an object is written. The other players have to guess who or what is on the card by asking up to 20 questions (such as 'Is it an animal?', 'Is it a vegetable?', or 'Is it big?') that can only be answered with a 'yes' or a 'no'.

Kim's Game Take a tray and arrange a selection of small objects on it, such as a spoon, a teacup, a brush, a thimble, some string and so on (about 10 items in total). Cover it with a tea towel and place the tray in front of the children. Explain that you will show them the contents of the tray for a couple of minutes and then you will cover it up. The children then have to write down all the items they can remember.

An alternative is to take the tray away, remove one item, then bring it back and ask the children to identify the item that is missing. Once children get the hang of this game they really enjoy it, and you will have to play several rounds. After a few rounds, add an object rather than removing one, and ask them to identify it, or swap an object and ask the players to identify its replacement.

outdoor games

What's the time Mr Wolf? Select one child to be Mr Wolf and stand him at one end of the garden with his back to his friends. Line all the other children up at the opposite end of the garden. Once ready, they shout, 'What's the time Mr Wolf?' The wolf can answer any time from one o'clock to twelve o'clock and the children can then take a step forward before asking again, 'What's the time Mr Wolf?'. The game continues until Mr Wolf shouts 'Dinner time!' and turns round and chases the children. The first one he catches then takes a turn at being the wolf.
Variation: The children take as many steps as the time the wolf gives: for three o'clock they take three steps, for nine o'clock, nine steps and so on.

Tug of war Draw two lines on the ground about 1 metre apart and mark the centre point between them. Take a length of rope and tie a hanky or streamer in the middle, and then arrange the two teams at either end of the rope an equal distance from the hanky, with the hanky hanging directly above the

RIGHT Apple bobbing can be messy, so you may want to provide something for each player to wear so that they don't get soaked.

BELOW LEFT Limbo dancing and a tug of war are both easily arranged and great fun.

central spot. The team that manages to pull the hanky across their line wins. A variation on this is the entire party against the birthday child's dad!

Limbo dancing You need a bamboo cane and two people to hold it: one at each end. The children then queue up and take it in turns to limbo-dance under the pole. Start with the pole at shoulder height. The children have to pass under the pole, leaning back without touching it. The winner is the person who successfully limbos under the pole at the lowest level.

Grandmother's Footsteps This is very similar to 'Mr Wolf', except that the children must try to creep up on the grandmother, who can turn around at any point. When she does, all the players must freeze. If anyone moves, they are sent back to the start line. The first child to reach grandmother takes her place, and the game starts again.

Apple bobbing This game is also good for indoor parties, but be warned that it can get very wet! Fill a large bucket with water and then drop in a few apples. Children take turns at trying to retrieve a floating apple with their teeth, while their hands are held behind their backs.

running races

Egg-and-spoon race Children run a race balancing an egg on a spoon. If they drop it they must return to the start. (You can use potatoes instead of eggs.)

Sack race Children step into sacks, which they hold up around their waists and then jump along a course.

Three-legged race Children run the course in pairs, with one of their legs tied to the other's at the ankle and their arms around each other for support.

Wheelbarrow race One child bends over with hands on the ground, the other child picks up their legs, and they proceed to run on their hands.

Balloon race Two teams line up and players pass a balloon from one to the other between their knees.

LEFT If you want to have a sack race, use bin bags or make your own sacks by sewing up old sheets or lengths of cheap fabric.

BELOW You don't have to waste real eggs on an egg-and-spoon race. Substitute potatoes, onions, stones or toy eggs instead.

the food

Parties are a time for fun and celebration, and it would be a miserable parent who stopped little Johnny and all his friends from enjoying a few sugary treats and salty snacks on his special day! Take this opportunity to set aside your anxieties about what your child should and shouldn't be eating, and concentrate instead on providing a feast that is fun, delicious and, above all, celebratory. That's not to say that you should feel obliged to abandon all your usual standards, but do bear in mind that this is a party, not an ordinary midweek supper, and so it's fine to go to town on the food. All the recipes in this section are quick, easy and delicious, and any assortment of them will provide you with a fantastic and healthy party meal that every child will enjoy.

crudités and dips

Houmous and guacamole served with breadsticks and veggie sticks make great finger foods for toddlers. Older children love these too, but make sure you offer a selection of breadsticks, crisps and pitta bread for those few children who will invariably turn up their noses at the sight of raw vegetables, however sweet and juicy.

crudités

carrot batons

cucumber batons

red pepper batons

celery batons

cherry tomatoes

blanched sugar snap peas or asparagus (cover with boiling water for 2 minutes, then drain under cold running water)

radishes

dippers

breadsticks, small or large

tortilla chips ('cool' flavour or the blue corn variety)

beetroot, carrot and parsnip vegetable crisps

mini oat biscuits or mini rice cakes

toasted pitta bread sliced into strips

bagel crisps
Slice 2 organic bagels widthways into 4 thin slices. Brush with a little olive oil, and then bake at 180°C (350°F) Gas 4 for 10 minutes. Break into pieces.

tortilla crisps
Cut 1 large flour tortilla into 8 slices. Place on a baking tray and cook at 180°C (350°F) Gas 4 for 10 minutes.

sweet potato wedges
Peel and cut 900g sweet potatoes into wedges. Place them in a roasting tin, toss in a tablespoon of olive oil, and sprinkle with a teaspoon of paprika. Cook for 35–40 minutes at 200°C (400°F) Gas 6, turning a few times. These are great with the sour cream dip below.

sour cream dip

150ml crème fraîche

2 spring onions, finely chopped

1 tablespoon lemon juice

SERVES 8

Lightly mix together all the ingredients. Don't over-stir, as the dip becomes runny quite quickly. This can be prepared the day before the party and kept in the fridge.

kid's guacamole

2 ripe avocados, halved and diced

2 tablespoons mayonnaise

1 teaspoon finely chopped fresh coriander leaves

2 tablespoons crème fraîche

SERVES 8

Put the avocado, mayonnaise and coriander in a food processor and whizz until smooth. Turn into a serving bowl and stir in the crème fraîche. Push the avocado stones into the mixture to prevent discoloration. Remove before serving. This will keep in the fridge for up to a day.

houmous

1 x 400g cans organic chickpeas, drained

juice of 1 lemon

75ml light tahini paste

2 tablespoons light olive oil, plus extra for drizzling

1 garlic clove, peeled and crushed

2 tablespoons boiling water

1 teaspoon sea salt

SERVES 8

Put the chickpeas and lemon juice in a blender and work to a smooth purée. Add the tahini paste, olive oil and garlic and blend until smooth. Scrape down the sides and add the boiling water. The consistency should be fairly loose and light. Taste and adjust seasoning if necessary, spoon into bowls and drizzle with a little olive oil. The houmous will keep in the fridge for a couple of days

tomato salsa

300g very ripe tomatoes

1 spring onions, finely chopped

1 garlic clove, peeled and crushed (optional)

1 tablespoon extra virgin olive oil

1 tablespoon chopped fresh basil leaves

1 tablespoon tomato ketchup

a little ground black pepper to taste

SERVES 8

Quarter and core the tomatoes and remove the seeds. Finely chop the tomatoes and put into a bowl. Add all the remaining ingredients and combine. Keep at room temperature until ready to serve. This will keep in the fridge for up to 3 days.

cookie-cutter sandwiches

Cookie cutters are an easy way of transforming a simple sandwich into something special. Make sandwiches no more than 2–3 hours ahead of the party; otherwise they'll go soggy.

ALL RECIPES SERVE 6-8 CHILDREN

Egg mayonnaise and cress
Shell 4 hard-boiled eggs and mash them in a bowl. Add 4 teaspoons mayonnaise and mix. Divide the mixture between 4 slices of bread, top with cress, and cover each slice with a second slice of bread. This is also a good filler for the pitta pockets (see below).

Banana and peanut butter
Spread 8 slices of bread with peanut butter. Slice 2 large bananas, place the slices on 4 of the slices, and cover with the other 4 slices.

pitta pockets

To freshen pitta bread, lightly sprinkle it with a little water then place in a toaster for a minute, cut it in half, and choose from one of the following filling suggestions.

ALL RECIPES FILL 6-8 HALVES OF PITTA BREAD

Tuna and carrot salad
Combine a drained 185g can of tuna with 2 coarsely grated carrots, 2 tablespoons chopped flat-leaf parsley and 2 tablespoons mayonnaise in a small bowl.

Cheese, bacon and tomato
Combine 50g coarsely grated cheddar cheese with 2 tablespoons crème fraîche, 2 chopped tomatoes and 4 rashers of crispy bacon, finely chopped.

Chicken and avocado salad
Combine 125g chopped chicken breast with 1 ripe avocado, 2 tablespoons crème fraîche, 1 tablespoon lemon juice, 1 tablespoon mayonnaise and 50g cos lettuce, shredded.

cheese straws

These taste delicious with the dips on pages 112–113, and can either be cut into giant straws for older kids or finger-length ones for toddlers. Cheese straws are popular with adults, too, so it's worth making two batches.

125g wholemeal flour, plus extra for dusting

55g butter, plus extra for greasing

85g Parmesan cheese, finely grated

1 egg yolk

2–3 tablespoons water

MAKES 20 SMALL STRAWS OR 10 GIANT STRAWS

Preheat the oven to 200°C (400°F) Gas 6. Lightly grease a baking tray.

Process the flour and butter together in a food processor until the mixture resembles fine breadcrumbs. Add two-thirds of the cheese and the egg yolk, and process in bursts until it comes together to form a ball. Flatten slightly, wrap and chill for 30 minutes.

On a floured surface, roll the dough out to a thickness of about 1cm and cut into long or short strips, depending on your preference. Lift onto the baking tray and sprinkle with the remaining Parmesan cheese. Bake for 10 minutes or until golden. Cool on a wire rack.

surprise burgers

Kids will enjoy helping to make these burgers – let them squelch the mixture into patties and hide a piece of cheese in the centre. The burgers can be made and frozen well ahead of time – just remember to defrost them well before cooking.

500g minced beef

2 teaspoons tomato sauce

1 tablespoon teriyaki sauce

4 spring onions, finely chopped

1 egg, lightly beaten

125g Cheddar cheese, cut into 8 small pieces

flour for dusting

vegetable oil for brushing

8 small part-baked bread rolls

tomato salsa to serve (see page 113)

8 small cos lettuce leaves

MAKES 8 BURGERS

Mix together the mince, sauces, spring onions and egg in a large bowl. With damp hands, divide the mixture into 8 balls, then shape into flat patties.

Insert a piece of cheese in the centre of each patty. Wrap the meat around the cheese and shape into a burger. Place on a lightly floured plate and chill for 30 minutes.

Brush the burgers with oil and cook on a cast-iron griddle pan or under a hot grill for 5–8 minutes on each side.

Meanwhile, bake the rolls according to the manufacturer's instructions. Split them in half and top the bases with the cooked burgers, tomato salsa and a lettuce leaf.

If you are cooking on a barbecue, place the burgers on a lightly oiled barbecue griddle over a medium heat, so they do not burn on the outside before being cooked through. Cook for 5–8 minutes each side.

finger-lickin' drumsticks

The marinade in this recipe is also great for pork chops or spare ribs.

4 tablespoons tomato sauce

4 tablespoons Worcestershire sauce

4 tablespoons dark brown sugar

2 tablespoons American mustard or Dijon mustard

8 chicken drumsticks or 16 chicken wings

125ml water

SERVES 8

For the marinade and dipping sauce, combine the sauces, sugar and mustard in a bowl. Divide the mixture into two.

Put the chicken legs or wings in an airtight plastic bag and pour in half of the sauce. Shake the bag, seal the end with a tie then put in the fridge for at least 3 hours.

Pour the remaining sauce into a pan, add the water and set aside.

Preheat the oven to 220°C (425°F) Gas 7. Remove the chicken from the bag and place in a baking dish. Cook for about 35–40 minutes, turning occasionally.

Bring the sauce to the boil for 5 minutes, then pour into a small dish. Remove the chicken from the oven and cool slightly before serving with the warm dipping sauce.

If you are cooking on the barbecue, scrape any excess marinade off the chicken legs and barbecue over direct heat for 40 minutes, turning occasionally.

corn on the cob

This sweet sauce makes corn on the cob more delicious than simply serving with melted butter.

2 large corn on the cobs

25g butter

4 tablespoons soft brown sugar

2 tablespoons water

SERVES 8

Cut the corn cobs into 3–4 cm sections. Cook in boiling water for 10–15 minutes or until tender.

Melt the butter, sugar and water in a large frying pan over a low heat. Add the cooked corn cobs and cook over a low heat gently for about 5 minutes, turning frequently to prevent the sugar from burning. Allow to cool a little before serving, as the caramel coating gets very hot.

If you are cooking on the barbecue, place each piece of cooked cob on a sheet of extra-thick foil, brush with the melted butter and sugar mixture, and sprinkle with a little water. Fold over the foil and seal to make a package. Place on a barbecue for about 10 minutes, turning occasionally.

crispy new potatoes

These potatoes become nicely roasted and crispy on the outside and make a great side dish that children love.

700g new potatoes, scrubbed

4 tablespoons olive oil

a little ground black pepper to taste

rosemary sprigs (optional)

2 tablespoons finely grated Parmesan cheese

bamboo skewers

SERVES 8

Preheat the oven to 200°C (400°F) Gas 6.

Toss the potatoes in a roasting tin with the oil, black pepper and rosemary. Roast them in the oven for 30-35 minutes, turning occasionally. Sprinkle over the grated cheese just before serving.

If you are cooking on the barbecue, cook the potatoes in a pan of boiling water for 10-12 minutes or until tender. Drain and return to the pan with the oil, black pepper and sprigs of rosemary (if using). Thread the potatoes on bamboo skewers that have been soaked in cold water for 30 minutes. Place on the a barbecue and cook over a medium heat for 7-8 minutes, turning regularly, until golden. Sprinkle over the grated cheese just before serving.

fruity coleslaw

Using a food processor fitted with a coarse grater will cut out the lengthy process of hand-grating.

350g white or red cabbage, coarsely grated

1 large carrot, coarsely grated

2-3 sticks celery, finely sliced

1 red dessert apple, cored and diced

1 ripe mango, peeled and diced

150ml mayonnaise

salt and a little ground black pepper to taste

SERVES 8

Combine the grated cabbage and carrot in a large bowl with the celery, apple and mango. Add the mayonnaise and season. Toss well to mix. Cover and leave to stand for 2-3 hours before serving. The coleslaw will keep in the fridge for a couple of days.

potato and mint salad

If you are serving fussy children, for a quiet life you might want to omit the mint leaves!

500g waxy or new potatoes, peeled and quartered

2 sprigs mint

100g frozen petits pois

half a lemon, squeezed

4 tablespoons extra virgin olive oil

a little ground black pepper to taste

SERVES 8

Put the potatoes in a pan with just enough boiling water to cover them. Add the mint and simmer for 10 minutes. Add the petits pois to the pan and cook for a further 5 minutes or until the potatoes are tender. Drain and discard the mint leaves.

When they are cool enough to handle, slice the potatoes and transfer them to a serving plate. Whisk together the lemon juice, olive oil and black pepper, and drizzle this mixture over the potatoes before serving.

garlic and herb bread

This healthy but tasty recipe uses less butter than 'normal' garlic bread.

3 cloves garlic, peeled and crushed

10g butter, very soft

3 tablespoons olive oil

1 tablespoon chopped flat-leaf parsley

1 tablespoon chopped fresh basil leaves

4 ciabatta rolls, split in half

MAKES 8 PORTIONS

Preheat the oven to 200°C (400°F) Gas 6.

Combine all the ingredients in a bowl and whisk, mixing well, until the butter and oil emulsify.

Spread each half-roll generously with the butter, place the two halves together, and wrap each roll in foil. Cook for 10-15 minutes.

If you are cooking on the barbecue, place the parcels on the barbecue over a medium heat for 10 minutes, turning once.

hot-dog howlers

Children love hot dogs. The sauce freezes well and can be made in advance.

HOT DOG SAUCE:

250ml water

1 small onion, finely chopped

80ml tomato ketchup

1 teaspoon mustard powder

1 teaspoon demerara sugar

1 teaspoon paprika (optional)

8 good-quality pork sausages

small milk rolls or wholemeal rolls

125g cheddar cheese, grated

MAKES 8 HOT DOGS

In a saucepan combine all the sauce ingredients. Bring to the boil and reduce the heat. Simmer for 5–10 minutes until thick and pulpy.

In a large frying pan, cook the sausages over a very low heat for about 20 minutes, turning occasionally until they are cooked through.

To serve, slice the rolls lengthways. Place a sausage in each roll, and top with the sauce and grated cheese.

rainbow popcorn

Popcorn can be made up to a day ahead, but make sure you store it in an airtight container so it stays crisp and fresh.

3 tablespoons vegetable oil

115g popcorn kernels

6 tablespoons runny honey

1 teaspoon each natural food colouring, such as beetroot, spinach and turmeric powder

50g butter

FOR THE CONES:

wrapping paper

sticky tape

MAKES ABOUT 8 CONES

Heat 1 tablespoon oil in a large pan over a high heat. Add a third of the corn kernels, cover and cook, shaking the pan constantly until all the kernels have popped.

Remove from the heat and transfer the popcorn to a large bowl. Add 2 tbsp honey, 1 teaspoon beetroot powder, and a third of the butter to the empty saucepan and melt together. Return a third of the popcorn to the pan and toss through the coloured butter, then set aside. Repeat the same process two more times, using the remaining honey and butter and the spinach powder and turmeric for colouring.

To make the paper cones, cut wrapping paper into 30cm squares and roll into cones. Secure with sticky tape.

sticky toffee apples

These do not work well made ahead of time, so make them on the day of the party.

12 small dessert apples	4 teaspoons lemon juice
12 wooden lolly sticks	4 tablespoons water
450g demerara sugar	colourful sprinkles
2 tablespoons golden syrup	MAKES 12 APPLES
60g unsalted butter	

Wash and dry the apples. Remove the stalks and push a lolly stick into the middle of each one.

Line a baking tray with oiled greaseproof paper.

Put the sugar, the syrup, butter, lemon juice and water into a heavy-based saucepan. Bring to the boil and, stirring the entire time, boil rapidly until the mixture reaches 140°C (275°F) or the 'soft crack' stage. If you don't have a thermometer, drop a teaspoon of toffee into a jug of cold water. If the toffee dissolves, it's not ready, but if it becomes stringy and separates into threads, it's ready. Take the pan off the heat and dip the base into a bowl of water to prevent the toffee from burning.

One at a time, dip the apples into the toffee until evenly coated. Stand the apples on the lined baking tray, scatter with sprinkles and leave to set in a cool dry place. They will keep for about 2 hours before the toffee becomes soft.

smoothie jellies

Using ready-made smoothies makes this recipe quick and easy.

5 sheets of leaf gelatine

700ml fruit smoothie

summer berries, to decorate

MAKES 8 JELLIES

Dissolve the gelatine according to the instructions on the packet. Once dissolved, combine the gelatine and the smoothie in a large jug and whisk.

Pour the mixture into individual wetted moulds and transfer to the fridge to set.

To turn out, quickly dip the containers in a bowl of warm water then invert onto plates. Decorate with berries. The jellies will keep for 2–3 days in the fridge.

jolly jelly boats

Children love these colourful little jelly boats.

3 large oranges

1 packet fruit-flavoured jelly

cocktail sticks

rice paper or coloured paper cut into sail shapes

MAKES 12 BOATS

Cut the oranges in half. Squeeze the juice, taking care not to pierce the skins. Make up the jelly according to the packet instructions. Place the orange shells on a baking tray and pour in the jelly mixture, making sure they are full to the top and the surface is level. Refrigerate until set.

Once set, cut the oranges in half again, using a sharp, wet knife. Pierce the paper sails with a cocktail stick and attach a sail to each jelly boat.

The orange halves can be made up to 2–3 days ahead of time and kept uncut in the fridge.

home-made ice lollies

Kids love lollies, and when made from fruit and yoghurt they are healthy as well as delicious. Ice-lolly moulds are available from kitchen shops or department stores. If you're short of time, you can also make ice lollies from ready-made smoothies.

orange and mango ice lollies

4 large ripe mangoes, peeled, stoned and roughly chopped

250ml freshly squeezed orange juice

MAKES 8–10 LOLLIES

In a food liquidizer, whizz the mango until smooth. Stir in the orange juice. Transfer the mixture to a jug, then pour into the lolly moulds. Press on the lids and transfer to the freezer overnight.

frozen fruit and yogurt lollies

2 x 420g pots of vanilla yoghurt

300g bag frozen mixed berries

2 tablespoons honey

MAKES 8–10 LOLLIES

In a food liquidizer or blender, whizz the yoghurt, berries and honey until smooth. Transfer the mixture to a jug, then pour into the lolly moulds. Press on the lids and transfer to the freezer overnight.

sparkling elderflower ices

500ml sparkling mineral water

100ml elderflower cordial

MAKES 12 SMALL LOLLIES

In a large jug, mix together the water with the cordial and stir until the mixture has dissolved. Transfer the mixture to a jug, then pour into the lolly moulds. Press on the lids and transfer to the freezer overnight.

knickerbocker glories

What child wouldn't want to get their hands on one of these? A tower of jelly and ice cream topped with a fizzing sparkler is the perfect end to any birthday meal.

1 packet strawberry jelly

1 packet lemon jelly

200g can peach halves, or 4 ripe peaches

200g can pineapple chunks, or 1 pineapple

500ml tub vanilla ice cream

142ml carton double cream, lightly whipped

8 fresh cherries and indoor sparklers for decoration

MAKES 8 SUNDAES

Make up the jellies according to the packet instructions; pour into shallow containers lined with clingfilm, cool, and refrigerate until set.

To assemble, chop the fruit into small chunks, then divide it equally between 8 glasses.

Invert the jellies onto a chopping board and roughly chop. Add a layer of strawberry jelly to each glass, then a layer of lemon jelly, then a scoop of ice cream. Finish off with a spoonful of whipped cream, a cherry and an indoor sparkler.

Light the sparkler and serve immediately, making sure the children stand well back until the sparkler has gone out.

virgin cocktails

The essential features of any children's cocktail are a dramatic name, vivid colour and fun accessories, including bendy straws, cocktail umbrellas and garnishes of fruit, such as pineapple, orange, banana, grapes and kiwi fruit. All these recipes can be made ahead of time and kept chilled in washed-out water or wine bottles. Label each bottle so you know which is which.

lemon silver bullet

4 unwaxed lemons

1.5 litres boiling water

4–6 tablespoons honey

1 litre chilled soda water

crushed ice

lemon and lime slices and cape gooseberries to decorate

MAKES 8 GLASSES

Using the thickest setting on the grater, grate the rind of each lemon down to the pith. Add the rind to the boiling water in a pan and simmer gently for 5–6 minutes.

Meanwhile, squeeze the lemons. Add the lemon juice, and honey to taste, to the pan. Stir until dissolved, pour into a jug and set aside to cool. Strain the mixture into a clean jug or bottle and discard the rind. Taste to check that it is sweet enough. Chill until ready to serve.

To serve, fill each glass two-thirds full with lemon drink, then top with soda water, crushed ice and lemon or lime slices.

tropical punch

175g sugar cubes

175ml boiling water

200g ripe mango or melon, peeled, seeded and chopped

juice of 2 limes and 2 lemons

500ml chilled orange or pineapple juice

500ml chilled sparkling mineral water

ice cubes to serve

MAKES 8 GLASSES

Stir the sugar and water together until the sugar has dissolved. Set aside to cool.

Put the mango or melon into a liquidizer and whizz until smooth. Pour into a jug with the sugar syrup and lime and lemon juice. Stir in the fruit juice and chill. To serve, top with mineral water. Serve in glasses half-filled with ice cubes.

strawberry apple slush puppy

500g strawberries, hulled

500ml chilled apple juice

juice of 2 limes or lemons

2 tablespoon caster sugar, or to taste

500ml crushed ice

1 litre chilled soda water, optional

strawberries to decorate

MAKES 8 GLASSES

Process the strawberries, apple juice, lime or lemon juice, sugar and crushed ice in a liquidizer until the mixture is slushy. Divide between tall glasses and top with soda water. Decorate and serve immediately.

chocolate hearts

These no-cook biscuits will keep in the fridge for up to a week, covered, or they freeze really well.

200g rich tea biscuits

130g butter

3 tablespoons golden syrup

2 tablespoons cocoa powder

50g raisins

50g hazelnuts, toasted, skinned and roughly chopped (optional)

100g milk chocolate

sugar flowers or icing sugar for decorating

MAKES 8-10 HEARTS

Butter a 20cm square tin.

Seal the biscuits in a plastic bag and smash into uneven crumbs with a rolling pin.

Melt the butter and syrup in a large pan. Stir in the cocoa powder, the raisins and the hazelnuts (if using), and finally the biscuit crumbs. Spoon the mixture into the tin, pressing down firmly. Melt the chocolate in a heatproof bowl over a pan of simmering water. Spread it over the biscuit base and chill for 1 hour. Cut into hearts or squares to serve.

Decorate with little pink sugar flowers or icing sugar.

mini fruit fondue

Make the fruit kebabs a day in advance and keep them in the fridge. The sauces can also be made ahead of time and kept in the fridge for 2 days.

WINTER FRUIT VERSION:

1 small pineapple, peeled, cored and cut into chunks

1 mango, peeled, stoned and cut into small chunks

2 banana, peeled cut into small chunks

SUMMER FRUIT VERSION:

125g strawberries, hulled

2 peaches, halved, stoned and cut into chunks

1 small cantaloupe melon, skin removed, deseeded and cut into small chunks

SWEET DIPS:

Greek yoghurt and honey mixed to taste

225g milk chocolate melted with 1 tablespoon of golden syrup

hundreds and thousands

cocktail sticks

MAKES 8 KEBABS

Thread 3 pieces of fruit onto each cocktail stick. Chill for 1 hour. Serve with the sweet dips.

choc-nut flapjacks

These extra-special flapjacks are studded with coconut, almonds and milk chocolate. Omit the nuts and chocolate if you prefer a plainer recipe. They will keep for 4–5 days in an airtight container.

125g butter

125g unrefined natural muscovado sugar

80g tablespoons golden syrup

210g porridge oats

25g desiccated coconut

30g whole almonds chopped into large chunks (optional)

glacé cherries (optional)

40g milk chocolate, roughly chopped

MAKES 12 FLAPJACKS

Preheat the oven to 180°C (350°F) Gas 4. Lightly butter a 23cm square cake tin and line the base.

Put the butter, sugar and syrup in a pan over a low heat until the butter melts and the sugar dissolves.

Remove from the heat and stir in the oats and coconut. Spoon into the tin and press down evenly.

Scatter over the almonds, and cherries (if using), and press lightly into the mixture. Bake for 15-20 minutes. Remove from the oven and immediately sprinkle over the roughly chopped chocolate. Set aside until cool.

Mark into bars or squares with a knife while still warm, then allow to cool before cutting through and removing the flapjacks from the tin.

jewel cookies

It is very important to bake these cookies on a clean non-stick baking tray, to prevent them from sticking. The cookies can be made ahead of time and stored in airtight containers.

140g butter, room temperature	200g plain flour, plus extra for dusting
100g natural unrefined icing sugar	30g ground almonds (optional)
1 drop vanilla essence	15 coloured boiled sweets
1 egg yolk	MAKES 20 COOKIES

Using a hand whisk, beat together the butter, icing sugar and vanilla until creamy. Add the egg yolk and beat well. Stir in the flour and ground almonds (if using) and quickly mix to a firm dough using your hands. Knead into a ball then lightly flatten. Wrap the dough in clingfilm and chill in the fridge for 2–3 hours.

Meanwhile, divide the sweets up into separate colours, place each colour into a plastic freezer bag and seal. Using a rolling pin, smash the sweets into tiny pieces. Set aside.

To bake the cookies, preheat the oven to 180°C (350°F) Gas 4 and grease two non-stick baking trays.

Turn the dough onto a lightly floured surface and roll out to a thickness of 5mm. Using assorted cookie cutters, cut into 7cm shapes. Cut out circles, triangles or diamonds in the centre of each biscuit, making sure you leave a generous margin around the sides.

Arrange on the baking trays and fill each hole with one colour of crushed boiled sweets. Bake for about 8 minutes, or until firm and light golden brown. Remove from the oven and allow the biscuits to settle for 1 minute before removing with a palette knife onto a cooling rack.

Helpful hint: if you allow the biscuits to cool for too long on the baking tray, they may stick. If this happens, put them back into a warm oven for a minute to allow the sugar to melt again.

star cookies

A sophisticated variation of the jewel cookies (see above) and perfect for a space party. Silver leaf is available from specialist cookware suppliers.

MAKES 20 COOKIES

Follow the recipe and method for the jewel cookies (see above), but after rolling out the pastry cut it into stars using a biscuit cutter.

To decorate with silver leaf, brush the surface of the biscuits with a paintbrush lightly dampened with cooled water. Allow the area to become tacky. Using tweezers, transfer pieces of silver leaf onto the star cookies to create a mottled silver effect.

gingerbread animals

Your kids can help cut out and decorate these cute animal cookies. They will keep for up to a week in an airtight container.

225g plain flour, plus extra for dusting	2 tablespoons unrefined dark brown sugar
1 teaspoon ground ginger	80g golden syrup
1 teaspoon ground cinnamon	1 tablespoon beaten egg
1 teaspoon bicarbonate of soda	icing sugar, coloured sugar, and hundreds and thousands to decorate
60g butter	MAKES 25 COOKIES

Preheat the oven to 190°C (375°F) Gas 5. Cover two baking trays with baking parchment.

Mix the flour, ginger, cinnamon and bicarbonate of soda together in a food processor. Add the butter and whizz until the mixture resembles fine breadcrumbs. Add the sugar, golden syrup and egg and blitz to form a soft dough. If it feels too dry, add a little more egg.

Roll the dough out to 5mm thickness. Using animal-shaped cutters, cut out and place the cookies on the baking trays. Bake for 8-10 minutes until light golden brown. Leave on the baking trays until firm, then transfer to a rack to cool.

To decorate the cookies, beat together 2 tablespoons icing sugar and a few drops of water to create a thin icing. Brush onto the surface of the biscuits and sprinkle with hundreds and thousands or coloured sugar.

butterfly cakes

These are very light fairy cakes with an unusual and delicious cream-cheese icing. The cakes freeze well undecorated, or make them ahead and store them in an airtight container.

1 tablespoon milk

3 eggs, lightly beaten

100g caster sugar

115g self-raising flour

85g butter, melted

CREAM-CHEESE ICING:

150g low-fat cream cheese

100g unrefined natural icing sugar

zest of 1 unwaxed lemon or orange, plus 2 tablespoons of juice

cake sprinkles and hundreds and thousands to decorate

MAKES 15 CAKES

Preheat the oven 190°C (375°F) Gas 5. Line a muffin tray with 15 paper cases.

Using an electric whisk, whisk the milk, eggs and sugar in a bowl until thick and glossy and doubled in bulk (it should leave a trail when the whisk is lifted). Add half the flour and half the butter and fold until evenly distributed, then fold in the remaining flour and butter. Using a tablespoon, fill the cases almost to the top. Bake for 10 minutes until risen and golden. Cool on a wire rack.

For the cream-cheese icing, beat together the cream cheese, icing sugar, zest and juice of the orange or lemon until smooth.

When the cakes are cool, slice a small circle off the top of the cakes, then cut it in half. Fill the hole with a little cream-cheese icing and push the two halves into the icing to form a butterfly shape. Decorate with sprinkles.

honey flake crunchies

Children will enjoy helping you make these. They freeze well, or will keep in an airtight container for up to a week.

15g butter

1 tablespoon runny honey

1 tablespoon demerara sugar

30g cornflakes

40g sultanas

MAKES 18 CRUNCHIES

Preheat the oven to 180°C (350°F) Gas 4. Line a muffin tray with 18 paper cases.

Melt the butter, honey and sugar in a small pan and stir over the heat until the butter has melted.

Add the cornflakes and sultanas and mix well. Divide the mixture between the paper cases.

Bake for 8-10 minutes or until lightly browned, remove from the oven, and allow to cool.

rocky road

These are full of forbidden treats, but wow do they taste good!

2 peanut or toffee chocolate bars, chopped coarsely

70g crisped rice cereal

100g small white marshmallows

75g roasted peanuts, unsalted

200g milk chocolate

1 teaspoons vegetable oil

MAKES 18 CASES

Line a muffin tray with 18 paper cases.

Mix together the chocolate bars, cereal, marshmallows and nuts in a large bowl.

Melt the chocolate and oil in a small pan over a low heat. Allow to cool slightly before pouring over the other ingredients. Mix well, then divide the mixture between the paper cases. Refrigerate for 30 minutes or until set.

party cakes

Although supermarkets sell celebration cakes of various kinds, nothing compares to a home-made cake – even if it is a little wonky or the icing dribbles. For the shaped and themed cakes in this section, use the recipe for Madeira cake. If you're short of time, buy several ready-made Madeira cakes and cut them into the shape you want before icing and decorating them as desired.

victoria sandwich

This classic cake recipe is perfect if you want a traditional circular, layered birthday cake. Decorate as simply or lavishly as you wish.

175g butter, softened	3 large eggs, beaten
175g naturally refined caster sugar	175g self-raising flour

Grease and line two 18cm sandwich tins.

Beat the butter and sugar together in a bowl until pale and fluffy. Add the eggs, a little at a time, beating well after each addition. Fold in half the flour, using a large metal spoon, then fold in the remainder.

Divide the mixture evenly between the tins and level the surface with a palette knife. Bake in the centre of the oven at 190°C (375°F) Gas 5 for about 20 minutes, until the cake has risen and springs back when lightly pressed in the centre. Loosen the edges of the cakes with a palette knife and leave in the tins for 5 minutes.

Turn out, remove the lining paper, invert and let cool on a wire rack.

Sandwich the cakes together with buttercream (see page 134). Make up the sugar icing for the top of the cake (see page 134). Pour the icing over the cake and decorate with dolly mixture, or other sweeties of your choice, and candles.

Variations:

Chocolate sandwich cake: Replace 45g flour with the same amount of cocoa powder. Sandwich the cakes together with vanilla or chocolate buttercream (see page 134).

Citrus sandwich cake: Add the finely grated zest of 1 orange or lemon to the mixture. Sandwich the cakes together with orange or lemon buttercream (see page 134).

Coffee sandwich cake: Blend 1 teaspoon instant coffee granules with 1 tablespoon boiling water. Cool and add to the creamed mixture with the eggs. Sandwich the cakes with vanilla or coffee buttercream (see page 134).

madeira cake

The secret of successful cake decoration is to use a firm, moist cake that can be cut and shaped without crumbling. Madeira cake is the best choice and can be flavoured for variety. The chart below shows three different quantities to allow you to create cakes of different sizes.

Bakeware	25cm square	30cm x 23cm	20cm round
Self-raising flour	375g	315g	250g
Plain flour	185g	155g	125g
Butter, softened	375g	315g	250g
Caster sugar	375g	315g	250g
Large eggs	6 eggs	5 eggs	4 eggs
Baking time	1 hour	45 minutes	50 minutes

Preheat the oven to 180°C (350°) Gas 4. Grease and line your cake tin.

Sieve together the flours. Put the soft butter and the sugar in a large mixing bowl, and beat until the mixture is pale and fluffy. Add the eggs gradually, alternating with 4 tablespoons of flour, until the mixture is light and fluffy. Add any flavouring required at this point. Using a large spoon, fold the remaining flour into the mixture.

Spoon the mixture into the prepared tin, then make a dip in the top of the mixture with the back of the spoon.

Bake in the centre of the oven for the appropriate time for the size of cake, until a skewer inserted in the centre comes out cleanly. Leave to cool for 10 minutes, then turn out and let the cake cool on a wire rack.

Madeira cake flavourings:

Vanilla: Add 1 teaspoon vanilla essence.

Lemon or orange: Add the grated rind and juice of 1 unwaxed lemon or 1 orange.

Chocolate: Add 2-3 tablespoons cocoa powder mixed with 1 tablespoon milk.

Almond: Add 1 teaspoon almond essence and 2-3 tablespoons ground almonds.

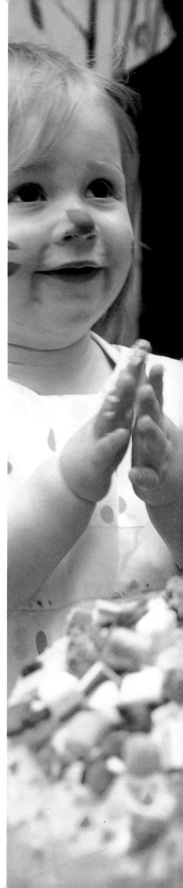

toppings and fillings

A thick, rich buttercream icing can hide a multitude of sins, from burned edges to sagging middles. And, of course, it's the icing rather than the cake that all the children adore.

buttercream icing

375g naturally refined icing sugar, sifted

125g butter, room temperature

1 tablespoon milk

MAKES ABOUT 450G

Place the butter in a mixing bowl or food processor. Add the milk and/or any flavouring. Sift the icing sugar into the bowl, a little at a time, beating after each addition, until all the sugar has been incorporated and the buttercream is light, fluffy and smooth.

Buttercream flavourings:

Vanilla: Add 1 teaspoon vanilla essence.

Lemon or orange: Add the zest of 1 unwaxed lemon and 1 orange. Replace the milk with 2 tablespoons freshly squeezed lemon juice or orange juice.

Coffee: Mix the milk and 1 tablespoon instant coffee powder to a paste and add to the buttercream.

Chocolate: Mix the milk and 2 tablespoons cocoa powder to a paste, and add to the buttercream.

other great toppings for cakes

Sugar icing A very simple icing, good for pouring over cakes and cookies. Mix together 225g sieved icing sugar with 2-4 tablespoons of hot water, and mix to the consistency of thin cream. Work quickly, as it will set fast.

Lemon drizzle topping Mix together 115g caster sugar with the juice of 1 lemon, stir until the sugar begins to dissolve, then pour over a freshly cooked cake.

Golden meringue frosting Perfect on a coffee cake. Put 175g naturally refined icing sugar, 1 egg white, a pinch of cream of tartar and 2 tablespoons of hot water in a bowl set over a pan of simmering water. Beat the mixture with an electric whisk for 10 minutes, or until thick and glossy.

mini fun cakes

These little cakes are a great alternative to a traditional birthday cake. Ice them to tie in with the party's theme, and arrange them on a plate to form a large square.

1 x 6 egg quantity of Madeira cake (see page 133)	food colouring (optional)
	icing pens in a variety of colours
2 x quantity of sugar icing (see opposite)	MAKES 25 MINI CAKES

Make a 25cm square Madeira cake (see page 133).

When the cake has cooled, cut it across and down into 25 small squares, each measuring approximately 5 x 5 cm.

Make the sugar icing and colour it with the food colouring of your choice (we used blue). Spread out the cake squares on a chopping board or cake board, and pour the icing over them, making sure you cover each one completely (make sure the icing is not too runny, or this will get very messy).

When the icing has set firm, place each mini cake in a paper case. Using squeezy icing pens (available from specialist cookware suppliers), decorate each mini cake with motifs that relate to the theme of your party.

If you are short of time, these mini cakes are easy to make from bought Madeira cake sliced up into smaller squares.

fantasy cakes

Making a cake to tie in with the theme of your child's party is easier than it looks. First, make your cakes, or buy ready-made Madeira loaves. Next, slice them to create the shape you want, using the cakes like building blocks and the buttercream icing as cement. The inevitable cracks will be hidden underneath the icing!

palace of dreams

A perfect cake for a beautiful princess! The cake can be assembled the day before the party.

3 x 5 egg quantity of
Madeira cake
(see page 133)

2 x 450g quantity of
buttercream
(see page 134)

5 ice-cream cones

cocktail sticks

rice paper or coloured
paper cut into flag shapes

dolly mixture and
marshmallows

Preheat the oven to 180°C (350°F) Gas 4.

Cook two quantities of Madeira cake in two 30 x 23cm greased and lined Swiss roll tins. These two cakes will form the base of the palace. Cook one quantity of Madeira cake in a 25cm greased and base-lined square tin. When cool, cut this square cake into five large squares and five smaller ones (these will form the turrets of the palace).

Colour two-thirds of the remaining buttercream with food colouring of your choice (we used blue). Colour the remaining buttercream in another colour (we used pink).

To assemble: Trim the edges of the two large rectangular cakes, then stack one on top of the other on a large cake board, 'glueing' the cakes together with buttercream.

Cover the base with blue buttercream. Position one large square on each corner and one in the centre at the back, and cover them with the blue buttercream.

Cover the smaller squares with the pink icing and place on top of the larger squares to form turrets. Top each turret with upturned ice-cream cones, and cocktail-stick flags. Then decorate the whole cake using mini marshmallows, sweets and sprinkles.

gingerbread house

Make the cake and gingerbread ahead of time and assemble the cake on the morning of the party.

1 x 6 egg quantity of Madeira cake (see page 133)

2 x 450g quantity of vanilla buttercream icing (see page 134)

1 x quantity of gingerbread mixture (see page 129)

White chocolate buttons, sweets, sprinkles, hundreds and thousands, bought gingerbread men, marshmallow wafers, chocolate roll wafers

Make a 25cm square Madeira cake (see page 133).

Trim the crust from the cake and slice the top flat. Cut the cake into four equal-sized squares and stack one on top of the other, making sure each layer is straight. Sandwich them together using buttercream as 'glue'. Trim a wedge from either side of the two top layers of cake to create a sloping roof effect.

Measure the sides of the cake, roll out half the gingerbread dough, and cut it to the same dimensions. Roll out the remaining gingerbread dough and cut two sides for the roof. Place the gingerbread pieces on baking trays and cook for 10-15 minutes at 190°C (375°F) Gas 5. Remove from the baking tray and place on a wire rack to cool.

To assemble: Trim the gingerbread pieces so they fit the sides and roof of the house. Spread a thick layer of buttercream over the surface of the cake and gently press the gingerbread in place.

Use the remaining buttercream to cover the roof, so it looks as though it is snow-covered. Decorate the sides using marshmallow wafers, white chocolate buttons, gingerbread men and women, chocolate roll wafers and little sweets.

choo-choo train

Believe it or not, this impressive train was made from three shop-bought Madeira cakes.

3 shop-bought Madeira
cake loaves

2 x 450g quantity of
buttercream icing
(see page 134)

sugar paste icing

tubes of different-coloured
icing

Constructing a birthday cake from bought Madeira cakes couldn't be easier. Simply cut them up and use them like building blocks to create the desired shape.

One cake was cut into thick slices to create the foundation of the cake. The back of the engine was carved from one whole cake, while the rounded front of the engine was carved from the other. The pieces of cake were glued together with apricot jam. If you are working on a more elaborate structure, you may need to use wooden skewers to hold the cake together; but make sure you don't forget to remove them before slicing the cake!

If you wish to use several different colours of icing, divide the buttercream between two or three bowls and add the desired food colouring. Decorate the cake with a thick layer of buttercream icing, using the different colours wherever desired. For the roof of the engine, roll out the sugar paste and cut to size. Using icing tubes, add window and door outlines and any other details you desire, then decorate using sweeties, chocolate buttons and liquorice wheels.

space shuttle

Fly them to the moon in this turbo-charged space shuttle. It can be assembled and decorated the day before the party, as long as it is kept in a cool place.

1 x 4 egg quantity
Madeira cake
(see page 134)

1 x 450g quantity of
buttercream icing
(see page 133)

4 or 5 shop-bought mini
sponge rolls

red and blue Smarties,
silver balls and liquorice to
decorate

orange or yellow sugar paste

Cook the Madeira cake mixture in a greased 1.2 litre ovenproof bowl for 50–55 minutes. Turn out and let cool. Trim the crust from the cake and slice the top flat. This will create the base of the spaceship.

To assemble: Using buttercream, stick together the sponge rolls. This will form the middle part of the ship. Place them on top of the base, then stick an upturned ice-cream cone on top of them to form the nose cone. Cover the whole cake with the remaining buttercream icing.

Place the cake on a round cake board and stick five ice-cream cones around the base to form the space shuttle 'legs'. Decorate the spaceship using blue and red Smarties, silver balls and liquorice wheels for portholes.

Roll out the orange sugar paste and cut into little triangles. Stick these around the base of the rocket and up around the sides to create a flame effect.

sources

PARTY TABLEWARE AND OTHER ACCESSORIES

CARGO HOME SHOP
Visit www.cargohomeshop.com or call 01844 261 800 for a catalogue or details of your nearest store.
Well-priced glasses, cookware, picnic stuff, and garden furniture.

HABITAT
Visit www.habitat.net or call 0870 411 5500 for details of your nearest store.
Funky tableware and napkins. Some small children's toys and novelty items at Christmas.

IKEA
Visit www.ikea.com for a catalogue or details of your nearest store.
Cheap and cheerful cookware, tableware and other kitchen accessories, such as ice trays, ice buckets and cocktail shakers.

PARTY PACKS
Visit www.partypacks.co.uk or call 01749 890634 for a catalogue.
Website and mail-order catalogue specializing in themed party decorations and tableware. They also sell a wide range of fancy-dress costumes, wigs, hats and excellent face painting kits, hook-a-duck games and even sacks for sack races, as well as balloons.

PARTYPIECES
Visit www.partypieces.co.uk or call 01635 201 844 for a catalogue.
Children's party website and mail-order catalogue, with sections devoted to themed tableware, small gifts, prizes, decorations and balloons. Also party games and costumes.

PARTY SUPERSTORE
268 Lavender Hill
London SW11 1LJ
020 7924 3210
www.partysuperstores.co.uk
Everything for every kind of party for children and adults. Party novelties, helium balloons, costumes to hire or buy, face paints, cake decorations, and tons of ideas for party bags.

THE PIER
Visit www.pier.co.uk or call 0845 609 1234 for details of your nearest store.
Decorative tableware from around the world as well as novelty cocktail items and fabric flowers.

URCHIN
Visit www.urchin.co.uk or call 0870 112 6006 for a catalogue
Mail order company with huge range of children's toys, funky tableware and a good selection of party accessories.

COSTUMES AND FANCY DRESS

BODEN
Visit www.boden.co.uk or call 0845 677 5000 for a catalogue.
Funky party outfits by mail order for boys and girls who don't want to wear costumes or fancy dress.

MAGGIE BULMAN COSTUME
020 8693 9733
Mobile: 07931 924 860
Email: maggie.bulman@virgin.net
www.enchantedcastle.co.uk
Imaginative children's costumes to buy or hire, many of which are featured in this book.

RACHAEL CAUSER
020 7639 8506
Maker of many of the costumes, accessories and props shown in this book.

FABRICS GALORE
52–54 Lavender Hill
London SW11 5RH
020 7738 9589
www.fabricsgalore.co.uk
Good selection of well-priced fabrics; fake fur, fleece, felts, prints, coloured muslins, ginghams and pretty dress fabrics.

PARTY STUFF ONLINE
www.partystuffonline.co.uk
Fancy dress for children, including clown outfits, suits of armour outfits, cowboy, cowgirl, squaw and Indian costumes, and fairy dresses with wings. Also themed party goods, balloons, colourful tableware and novelties.

COOKWARE AND CAKE DECORATING

CUCINA DIRECT
Visit www.cucinadirect.co.uk or call 0870 420 4311 for a catalogue.
Brilliant catalogue for the keen cook, with lots of shaped baking trays and moulds.

HOPE AND GREENWOOD
20 North Cross Road
London SE22 9EU
020 8613 1777
www.hopeandgreenwood.co.uk
Old-fashioned sweets and confectionery.

KNIGHTSBRIDGE PME
www.cakedecoration.co.uk
Fantastic selection of cake-making accessories. Silicone moulds in every shape imaginable, including unicorns and butterflies, and the tin mould for the star cookies shown on page 32. Also a wide selection of icing tubes, icing writing pens, ready-made fondant icing, sparkling sugar, decorative sprinkles and coloured sugar paste.

DAVID SHUTTLE
9 The Broadway
Penn Road
Beaconsfield
Bucks HP9 2PD
01494 677 665
www.davidshuttle.com
Unusual cake sprinkles, butterfly, flower, sun, animal and medal cutters, pretty paper cake cases and coloured sugar.

THE SPICE SHOP

1 Blenheim Crescent

London W11 2EE

0207 221 4448

www.thespiceshop.co.uk

Natural food colourings such as beetroot powder and spinach powder for the coloured popcorn recipe on page 120.

SQUIRES KITCHEN

3 Waverley Lane

Fanham

Surrey GU9 8BB

01252 711749

www.squires-group.co.uk

Everything related to cake decorating and sugarcraft, including cake tins, cakeboards, silver and gold leaf, food colouring, sugar pastes, icing in tubes and mini cutters. Also a classic sweet shop stocking jellybeans and old-fashioned favourites.

DECORATIONS AND PROPS

DZD

145 Tottenham Court Road

London W1T 7NE

020 7388 7488

www.dzd.co.uk

Fantastic source of background props at trade prices. Foliage, anchors, clouds, suns, ships' wheels, treasure chests, flower garlands, net butterflies, Christmas decorations, lights, paper decorations and much more in their extensive catalogue.

THE HOLDING COMPANY

243–245 King's Road,

London SW3 5EL

020 7352 1600

www.theholdingcompany.co.uk

Storage ideas for kids – lunch boxes of all shapes and sizes, and fun storage ideas for bedrooms.

PAPERCHASE

213 Tottenham Court Road

London W1P 7TS

020 7467 6200

Visit www.paperchase.co.uk for details of your nearest store.

Funky stationery, art and craft materials and novelty gifts.

PURVES AND PURVES

www.purves.co.uk

Children's section full of quirky toys and outdoor equipment, all with an emphasis on good design.

WIN GREEN

www.wingreen.co.uk

Fabric playhouses in many designs – there is a gingerbread cottage, a sheriff's office, a knight's castle, a fairy hanging tent and a circus big top. Also tablecloths, beanbags, cushions and bunting.

GOING-HOME PRESENTS AND PARTY PRIZES

ECOTOPIA

www.ecotopia.co.uk

Children's toy website for the green-minded

GRACE AND FAVOUR

35 North Cross Road

London SE22 9ET

020 8693 4400

Interior accessories and toys and baby clothes with a vintage feel

THE GREAT LITTLE TRADING COMPANY

Visit www.gltc.co.uk or call 0870 850 6000 for a catalogue

Dressing-up boxes containing a selection of outfits, as well as pirate chests and activity kits.

LETTERBOX

Visit www.letterbox.co.uk or call 0870 6007878 for a catalogue.

Mail-order company with good selection of small party-bag treats as well as fancy dress costumes, toy storage and personalized gifts, including bunting.

MUJI

Visit www.muji.co.uk for details of your nearest store.

Cute stationery and travel-sized toiletries for party bags.

MULBERRY BUSH LTD,

Visit www.mulberrybush.co.uk or call 01403 754 400 for a catalogue.

An excellent range of traditional gifts and toys. Good source of birthday presents and nice prizes.

PRIMARK

Visit www.primark.co.uk for details of your nearest store.

Accessories and bits and pieces for party bags, especially for girls. Also cheap clothing that can be customized for costumes.

RED HOUSE

Visit www.redhouse.co.uk or call 0870 191 9980 for a catalogue.

Brilliant children's book website and catalogue offering a huge selection of current publications at reduced prices. Particularly good for bulk-buying books for going-home presents.

TOYS R US

Visit www.toysrus.co.uk for details of your nearest store.

Toy superstores that stock all the latest 'must-have' toys and gadgets as well as a selection of pocket-money toys suitable for going-home presents. Also a good selection of outdoor playhouses and climbing frames.

THE WOODEN TOY CATALOGUE

Visit www.woodentoysonline.co.uk or call 0870 027 3495 for a catalogue.

Traditional wooden toys, games and puppets, with a section devoted to pocket-money toys suitable for party bags.

WOOLWORTHS

Visit www.woolworths.co.uk for details of your nearest store.

High-street store with excellent selection of toys, stationery and novelties that are ideal for party bags. Also some dressing-up costumes, party tableware, cards and gift wrap.

picture credits

ALL PHOTOGRAPHY BY POLLY WREFORD

Key: a=above, b=below, r=right, l=left, c=centre.

Endpapers: balls from Purves & Purves; 1 plastic eggs and hens from DZD; 2 girl left costume by Rachel Causer, boy centre and girl right costumes by Maggie Bulman, glasses from The Pier, cake stands from Grace & Favour; 6l cushion from Grace & Favour; 6r pirate accessories from Party Superstore; 6b sheriff's hut from Win Green; 7ac crown from Party Party; 7bc house on stilts from The Great Little Trading Company; 7ar ball from Purves & Purves; 7br cowboy hat from Party Superstore; 8 bowl and plate from Purves & Purves, cutlery from Habitat; 10al clown and pirate accessories from Party Superstore; 10cl glass from Ikea; 10bl plastic eggs from DZD; 10ar ship's wheel from DZD; 12-17 Teddy Bears' Picnic: bear costume by Maggie Bulman, pavilion from Win Green, bowls and plates from Purves & Purves, cushions, blanket, basket and flask from Grace & Favour, bunting and sandpit from Urchin, tea set from Toys r Us ; 18-23 Farmyard Animals: bunnies, hens, butterflies, caterpillars and paper flowers from DZD; cushions from Win Green; cardboard house from Ecotopia; 24b soldier skittles from Grace & Favour; 26-31 Under the Sea: octopus and mermaid costumes by Maggie Bulman, paper hair and crown by Rachel Causer, hanging storage, table, chairs, glasses and cups from Ikea, net and fish mobiles from DZD, all paper from Paperchase, glass cake stand from Grace & Favour, balloons from Party Superstore; 32-37 Fairies: balloons from Paperchase, mosquito net from The Pier, cake stand from Urchin, shell bowl from Grace & Favour, paper cups and bowls from Party Superstore, cushion from The Pier; 38-43 Pirates: ship's wheel, treasure chest, rope and skull from DZD, pirate balloons and pirate accessories Party

Superstore, pirate flags by Maggie Bulman, pirate costumes 40al, 40bl, 41 & 43a girl on left all by Maggie Bulman; 44c chocolate money from Hope & Greenwood; 45bl skull and rope from DZD; 46-51 Wild West: tableware from Purves & Purves, red cushion from Grace & Favour; cowboy hats and accessories from Party Superstore, cowboy laundry bag by Emily Medley, sheriff's hut from Win Green, wigwam from The Great Little Trading Company; 46, 48a & 50bl cowboy, cowgirl and squaw costumes by Rachel Causer; 47al, 50al & 50-51 chief and squaw costumes by Maggie Bulman; 52-57 Circus: straws, face paints and circus accessories from Party Superstore, basket from Habitat, tiger fabric, fabrics for tent and awning from Fabrics Galore, rug from Ikea, sweets and wrapping paper from Hope & Greenwood, pink bowl and spotty apron from Cucina Direct, cake stands from Urchin, table cloth from The Pier, paper cups from Sainsbury's, folding table from Paperchase, all circus costumes by Rachel Causer; 58-63 Space: cardboard rocket from Ecotopia, space wall decoration and mobile from Ikea, spaceman costume by Rachel Causer, alien costume Maggie Bulman; 64-69 Knights and Princesses: sword, shield and gold crown from Party Superstore, sugar paper for banners and knight toy from Toys r Us, paper for shelf trim and torch flames from Paperchase, costumes by Maggie Bullman, 69al head-dresses by Rachel Causer; 70a crown from Party Superstore; 70b space hoppers from Purves & Purves; 71ar spaceman costume by Rachel Causer; 71br alien costume by Maggie Bulman; 72-77 Tropical Island: paper cocktails, paper garland swags, giant palm leaves and parrot from DZD, cocktail parasols and tree, floral cushions and lanterns from The Pier, plastic glasses, jug on table and table shades from Cargo Home Shop, neck garlands and grass skirts from Party Superstore, 72ar Boy's Hawaiian shirt from Mini Boden;

78-83 Gangsters and Molls: 78 girl left and boy right costumes by Maggie Bulman, girls centre left and right by Rachel Causer, boy centre costume from Party Superstore, 79 spats by Maggie Bulman, ice-cream glasses from Cargo, glasses and straws from The Pier, paper and card for decorations and cube holders from Paperchase, glass cake stand from Grace & Favour; 85al swizzle sticks from The Pier; 86-91 all card and paint from Paperchase; 92 wrapping paper from Woolworths, bags from Paperchase; 93 pots from Muji, pencils from Paperchase; 94bl fabric from Fabrics Galore; 95a boxes from Ikea; 95b pencil toppers from Woolworths; 96l baskets from Habitat, flowers from Primark; 96r watering cans from Ikea; 97 pots from Paperchase; 987al bags from Primark; 99 hatboxes from The Holding Company; 101 bin from The Holding Company; 110 sauce squeezers from Purves & Purves, spotty plates and cocktail sticks from The Pier; 112-113 orange dip plates from Purves & Purves; 114 cardboard packed lunch boxes from Party Superstore; 116-117 wooden plates from Purves & Purves; 118-119 bowls from Purves & Purves; 120 popcorn bowl from Cucina Direct; 122a plate from Purves & Purves; 123 paper wig made by Rachel Causer; mould for lollies from Cucina Direct; 124-125 mini sparkler from Paperchase, tablecloth from The Pier; 126 heart mould from Cucina Direct; 130-131 spotty tray and bowls from The Great Little Trading Company; 132 bunting from Urchin, fabric on table from Fabrics Galore; 134a plate from Purves & Purves; 136-137 fabric on table from Fabrics Galore. All the paper, card, glue, sticky tape, glitter, and other craft materials used in this book came from Paperchase.

index

Page numbers in italics
indicate captions

acknowledgments

We would like to thank the following people for all their hard work and support over the past six months: Andrew Treverton, for whom no task was too big or small, and who was on call night and day cutting, pasting, carrying and building; Vicky Robinson, who helped bring our ideas to life; Rachael Causer, who made so many wonderful costumes, invitations and decorations; Maggie Bulman, for the loan of her beautiful fancy dress costumes and for arranging many of the models; Hattie Berger, for all the play dough and her failsafe recipe; the team at Ryland Peters & Small, for all their help and enthusiasm; Polly Wreford, for her gorgeous photographs which captured so perfectly the mood we wanted.

Thanks should go to all our models and guinea pigs, without whom the book would not have been possible: Angelica, Arthur, Beatrice, Betty, Blaise, Charlie, Christian-Ray, Dylan Jacob, Eden, Edie, Eliza, Erin, Esme, Florence, Florrie, Fred, George, Grace, Gus, Hal, Harry, Jacob, Jacob-Jobe, James, Joelle, Kitty, Leila, Lily, Linus, Luke, Martha, Matilda, Max, Maya, Megan, Millie, Mitsy, Molly, Pearl, Reece, Rosa, Sam, Scarlet, Tilda, Til and Yasmin.

Thank you also to all the location owners, who allowed us to turn their homes into party venues.